Christian, Be Free

Christian Be Free

SAMUEL PESTES

Tyndale House Publishers, Inc. Wheaton, Illinois

Unless otherwise noted, Scripture quotations are from the King James Version. Other quotations are from *The Amplified Bible* (Amp.), © 1965 by Zondervan Publishing House; the *New American Standard Bible* (NASB), © 1960, 1962, 1963, 1968, 1971 by The Lockman Foundation, La Habra, California; the *New International Version* (NIV), © 1978 by New York International Bible Society, and *The Living Bible* (TLB), © 1971 by Tyndale House Publishers.

Library of Congress Catalog Card Number 80-53243. ISBN 0-8423-0251-4, paper.

First printing, February 1981. Printed in the United States of America.

CONTENTS

INTRODUCTION

Excitement and a sense of expectancy was evident as the people began to arrive and started settling in for the yearly Bible conference.

Well-to-do people, enjoying the best the world had to offer, as well as poor and sick people—all came with varying degrees of hope and anticipation.

Some attended the annual assembly eager to hear speakers whom they hoped would lift their spirits. Others came because loyalty to the church demanded their presence at such an important organizational function. Some, especially the younger generation, were drawn by the desire to meet other young people of the same faith.

As a Seventh-day Adventist pastor, and chairman of the locating committee for the conference, I had an opportunity to get close enough to the people as they arrived to become acquainted with their needs and what they hoped to get out of the conference. Their smiling faces and expressions of well-being often hid heartaches and pain accumulated through the years. Some, rather than finding answers to their needs, had learned to suppress and ignore problems which seemed to have no solution.

During the ten days of the conference, my wife Dorothy, who served as camp nurse, was on call twenty-four hours a day. Demands on her time were so heavy that she found it difficult to attend all the meetings. People with physical ailments sought help from the medical team; those with emotional and spiritual problems were referred to professional counselors and pastors. Everyone seemed to be working for the same overall goals, creating a sense of comradeship that was in itself enough to make the conference seem worthwhile for some of us.

As each group arrived during the opening day, we could sense the burdens weighing on the people—young and old. Then as the conference continued, we realized that some of the changes and answers they sought weren't coming. As Dorothy and I discussed the needs we were seeing, we realized how difficult it was for the conference workers to treat more than just the symptoms.

As the week progressed, the speakers preached well, encouraging the people with stories of miracles occurring on the mission fields during the past year. But very little was being said about the victorious life God had promised through the gifts of the Holy Spirit.

Our church leaders seemed to feel that the other Christian groups were overemphasizing the miraculous and the spectacular to the exclusion of other more routine and down-to-earth prophetical and doctrinal truths. Because of that overemphasis, our church tended to lean the other way, stressing the objective doctrinal truths as we understood them to the exclusion of the subjective expressions and experiences. Much more emphasis was being placed on the miracle of salvation than on how a person could sustain a daily walk in the power of the Holy Spirit.

We were careful about how we spoke of miracles. The Bible says that in the latter days evil spirits will perform miracles by which they will deceive, if it were possible, even the elect (Mark 13:22). In the light of this verse, we were somewhat wary of miracles. However, it now occurred to us that in trying to avoid one possible error we were possibly insulating ourselves from something good that God intended for us to have.

Jesus' ministry was full of miracles. The apostles were given miracle-working powers to give authority to their preaching. After all, what would have been the point of a sermon about spiritual healing if no one could demonstrate it physically? When Peter preached on the power of God to do the impossible, the people who heard his sermon did not have to wonder what he was talking about. Signs and miracles followed them that believed (Mark 16:20).

When Peter saw the lame man begging at the temple gate, he knew exactly what God wanted him to do and he did it. As the Holy Spirit impressed upon him to minister to the man, Peter received a boldness which shut out any trace of doubt or fear. He did not pray for the man, nor did he try to prepare him psychologically in case God didn't heal him. Peter knew at that instant that God wanted him to demonstrate that same power to raise this man as Jesus had used in raising Lazarus. He knew that the responsibility was God's and not his. When the word was spoken, the impossible happened, and the man became a living visual aid of what God could do. When the people saw that God was Master in the physical realm, they gained confidence to entrust their souls to him. Unfortunately, many today are afraid that when they ask God for bread, they may find themselves holding a stone. Because they feel that way, they can't see themselves resting in the arms of a loving heavenly Father.

Many have conditioned themselves not to accept anything by faith before their rationality gives assent. Thus their capacity to understand sets the limit beyond which even God will not help them. Such lives are not founded basically upon faith but upon their understanding. Adam and Eve faced the same problem in the Garden of Eden; they had to choose to live by faith and trust God completely or choose to depend on their own mental abilities and understanding of what they thought was best for them. We began to think that many of our conference guests were operating on that spiritual level.

As the conference wore on, we seemed as a group to be living in the shadow of the New Testament gospel rather than in its light. We felt so helpless. I confessed to Dorothy that, even though my own ministry projected a form of godliness, it seemed to lack the power thereof (2 Tim. 3:5).

The conference ended without any overwhelming evidence of anything extraordinary except the miracle of salvation to which many professed. To many of the people who were suffering from spiritual problems, God still seemed impersonal and remote. "Why were so many of us not living up to our potential as sons and daughters of God?" I wondered.

During the following months, I spent many hours searching for answers to that question. Having implicit confidence in the writings of my church's founders, I began to study the books of Ellen G. White with renewed zeal. Volume one of *Testimonies to the Church* proved especially helpful because there I found recorded some of the experiences of our Seventh-day Adventist pioneers. As I read about the ministry of the Holy Spirit among those early men and women of God, I recognized very little similarity between what was happening within our church then and now.

I read that on numerous occasions when they met for prayer that the sense of God's presence was among them in most unusual ways. As in the days of Daniel, Isaiah, John, and the other disciples, when these pioneers met to worship, they were often smitten to the ground by the sense of God's nearness.

On one occasion, as the book recorded, a whole prayer group felt physically immobilized by God's power throughout the night until they were found the next morning by neighbors. Numerous healings and miracles of all kinds were said to occur among these believers. They knew God was alive, not merely because they gave mental assent to what the Bible said, but because they were experiencing him day by day.

Even though I was not psychologically or theologically prepared to accept the idea of such peculiar behavior, I realized those people must have known God in a very personal way. I became desperately hungry for such a vital relationship with God. I was especially concerned to know why the Holy Spirit, the Spirit of Prophecy, seemed no longer operative in our midst. Paul wrote that God's people would experience the indwelling of the Holy Spirit (1 Cor. 3:16).

The Seventh-day Adventist position was (and still is) that their church is a special vehicle of the Spirit of Prophecy because he was present in the lives of the early church pioneers and that the church remains the custodian of these early believers' writings. I did not realize at the time how much this belief was hindering my spiritual growth. To my knowledge, no individual church in the whole conference would claim to have that same kind of ministry of the Holy Spirit in their midst. Yet we boasted that the Seventh-day Adventists were identified as the church through which the Spirit of Prophecy is ministering. We quoted Revelation 12:14 in support of our claim, but overlooked the inditement of Revelation 3:17, 18:

> Because thou sayest, I am rich, and increased with goods, and have need of nothing; and knowest not that thou art wretched, and miserable, and poor, and blind, and naked; I counsel thee to buy of me gold tried in the fire, that thou mayest be rich; and white raiment, that thou mayest be clothed, and that the shame of thy nakedness do not appear; and anoint thine eyes with eyesalve, that thou mayest see.

Deeply concerned over the condition I was seeing in our church, I turned to the Bible for help and comfort. The promise of Jesus that he would never leave us nor forsake us gave me the courage to hope. But the knowledge that I also was living beneath my potential troubled me like a sore that would not heal. One day I read Hebrews chapter six and the warning of that message seemed directed straight at me:

> Therefore let us go on and get past the elementary stage in the teachings and doctrine of Christ, the Messiah, advancing steadily toward the completeness and perfection that belongs to spiritual maturity. Let us not again be laying the foundation of repentance and abandonment of dead works [dead formalism], and of the faith [by which you turned] to God, with teachings about purifying, the laying on of hands, the resurrection from the dead, and eternal judgment and punishment. [These are all matters of which you should have been fully aware, long, long ago.] If indeed God permits we will [now] proceed [to advanced teachings]. For it is impossible [to restore and bring again to repentance] those who have been once for all enlightened, who have consciously tasted the heavenly gift, and have become sharers of the Holy Spirit, and have felt how good the Word of God is and the mighty powers of the age and world to come, if they then deviate from the faith and turn away from their allegiance; [it is impossible] to bring them back to repentance, for (because, while, as long as) they nail up on the cross the Son of God afresh, as far as they are concerned, and are holding [Him] up to contempt and shame and public disgrace. [Heb. 6:1-6, Amp.]

These words made me realize that either I had to move on to Christian maturity, or I would be in danger of sinning against the Holy Spirit by my refusal to advance with him. I saw as never before that to displease the Lord I did not necessarily have to turn my back on Christ, and head back into the world, but simply refuse to move on to maturity. Even as it was necessary for the Israelites to move on when the pillar of fire moved, if they hoped to continue with

God's blessings, I had to move on to maturity as the Lord led me.

This is the story of how God lifted Dorothy and me out of our dilemma and gradually emptied us of all that had cluttered our minds and prevented our becoming useful vessels for him. Before he could fill us with the new wine, he had to prepare us as new bottles. Perhaps God may use this record of his work in our lives to lead you on into his Rest, and that you may also cease from your work and begin to glorify God in the finished work of Christ.

1
Working—Not Resting

I was born and raised on a farm by devout Seventh-day Adventist parents. We attended church as regularly as the prairie roads to our isolated farm in western Canada would permit. Each of the six children left the roots of our farm home, attended church-related schools, and each graduated from some course in higher education.

I had an eager mind, but was never unsettled about the "faith of our fathers." It was not until my calling as a minister thrust me out into the field of ministry that I became painfully aware of a great lack of spiritual power with which to fulfill such a task. Out of this deep personal need rose the questions that initiated my search for something better.

My call to the ministry had come in a very clear, definite way so that I literally left my plow and the farm which was to have been my inheritance, and enrolled in Bible college. During my senior year, the Lord confirmed this call through the dean, the board, and certain professors at the school, who met with each of us to help us decide what our future ministries should be.

I graduated from Walla Walla College with a bachelor's degree in theology, and soon after I was married to a wonderful nurse, who was the answer to my prayers for a life companion. Together we began an internship, assisting an evangelist in Nanaimo, British Columbia. There we worked for about a year, after which we were given our first assignment on our own. Our desire to be soul-winners and our youthful enthusiasm created such excitement within us that we felt like shouting, "Prince Rupert—get ready; here we come!" We could hardly wait to begin our work as co-laborers with God. We were at that time confident enough to tackle any assignment they would have given us, however great or small.

Prince Rupert, the city we were sent to "open up," lies just south of the Alaskan panhandle. Nine hundred miles of circuitous, barely passable roads were the only practical land link between Vancouver and this west coast port at that time. Because of the rough trip, I sent Dorothy, almost due with our first baby, ahead by boat, accompanied by her mother.

I hitched our first very own home, an old and heavily-built twenty-eight-foot house trailer, to our 1947 six-cylinder Pontiac and began, all alone, the most demanding journey that either my faith or strength had ever known. Dorothy and I were both Christians—we knew Jesus as our Savior from sin, but we were still unaware of all the spiritual inheritance available to us. Four years of working my way through school, carrying a heavy study load, had taught me some valuable lessons of reliance upon God. I didn't realize that on this wilderness road God was going to give me many more tests to prove my trust and strengthen my relationship with him.

LEARNING TO REST

I remember pulling out of Vancouver in a driving rain, which had turned all the gravel roads into a jumble of ruts and potholes. Further north the trail continued to worsen until it was impossible to move faster than ten to fifteen miles per hour for fear of breaking an axle or spring. The smooth purr of the newly-tuned engine gave a feeling of security as I drove hour after hour in the near-freezing rain.

My first unscheduled stop was at Cache Creek, about two hundred miles out of Vancouver. An erratic, swaying motion of the trailer had alerted me to a problem. On examining the trailer, I found that a couple of rivets remaining on a broken wheel were all that was holding it together and keeping the lurching trailer from falling upon its axle.

I pulled into the biggest service station in Cache Creek and inquired about a replacement for my antique LaSalle trailer wheel. The amused manager replied, "You won't find a wheel like that this side of Vancouver."

Glancing over a large pile of automobile junk stashed behind the garage, I asked permission to look around. "Help yourself; but you're wasting your time," the manager said. "In fact, if you can find one, you can have it free."

Breathing a prayer, I turned some junk over and uncovered something that looked suspiciously like a twin to the broken trailer wheel. Checking the number of bolt holes, and the distance between them, confirmed my hopes. This was my wheel! Incredulous, the station manager looked at it and muttered, "I never saw that wheel before."

As he helped me install it, I rejoiced, because I knew that God had somehow arranged to store just the part I needed for this moment. The man refused payment, and as he waved me on, he said, "Good luck, fellow. You'll need it."

I knew what had happened wasn't luck but providence. I thought of the verse I'd read many times: "Casting all your care upon him; for he careth for you" (1 Pet. 5:7). "Thank you, Father," I said. "Please watch over me, and take me safely to my family waiting in Prince Rupert."

Perhaps it was best that I did not know that it was going to take four more days of driving twenty hours a day to cover the remaining seven hundred miles over treacherous roads.

On the third day, while climbing a steep mountain grade,

my car tires lost traction and spun out of control on the gravel road. Both house trailer and car slipped back down the hill and narrowly escaped plunging into the canyon. One rear wheel started over the edge of the precipice. I must have looked like a one-man band with a foot on the car brake, one hand squeezing the electric brakes, and the other hand honking the horn as often as the power-drained battery would permit.

After hanging onto the brakes for what seemed like an eternity, my arms and legs began to cramp. Fear gripped my heart as I realized I might be the only person within fifty miles of that lonely spot. Thoughts and heart raced together into panic as I cried out to God. Satan's attack upon my mind during those moments was almost overwhelming.

Perched high on that mountainside, with a sheer wall of rock on my right and a chasm on my left, I was the perfect picture of helplessness. The swift-flowing Fraser River below seemed like a yawning serpent waiting for its prey, while the wall on my right seemed to be crowding me off the trail. The mountains in the distance were looking and waiting for the next act of the drama, and nearby a hammering woodpecker marked off the seconds as the countdown continued. I knew that in a few more minutes I would have to jump and let everything we owned go over the edge and into the waiting river.

Then the Lord brought to pass what he had promised. "But God is faithful, who will not suffer you to be tempted above that ye are able" (1 Cor. 10:13). A new sound began to disturb the perfect stillness of that wilderness. Soon I recognized it as the rumble of a large truck coming in my direction. I watched the logger extend a chain from his truck to the front end of my car. He warned that there would be no alternative but to start with a quick jerk because the road was too steep for a steady pull.

On the first lunge, the logging chain snapped like a string. He quickly repaired the broken link with a bolt, and shouted to keep my door open so I could jump if he should happen to pull the front end out of the car. Language failed as I tried to pray, and for the first time I felt my need of the Holy Spirit's intercession to pray with "groanings that cannot be uttered" (Rom. 8:26).

Horrified, I watched the front end of the car rise into the air. Relief flowed over me like soothing ointment as the wheels settled down again and we began to inch forward. The hail of gravel hitting my windshield from the spinning truck tires only brought more shouts of encouragement for him to "Keep moving, keep moving!"

Arriving safely at the crest of the mountain, I was speechless as my benefactor and I shook hands. He refused any reward beyond a "thank you," saying that I could repay him by helping another fellow traveler in need. His parting words were "I wish you luck. There's a much worse hill ahead."

"What a comforting thought," I sighed. Thoughts of another verse came to mind: "This poor man cried, and the Lord heard him, and saved him out of all his troubles. The angel of the Lord encampeth round about them that fear him, and delivereth them" (Ps. 34:6, 7).

I was grateful to be on the road again, but dreaded the big hill the truck driver said was ahead. It was a relief to have a few hours of uneventful travel. Then in the late afternoon, when slowing to negotiate a sharp turn onto a narrow curving bridge, I saw that the road beyond turned abruptly again up a steep and winding grade. I had driven through mountains before, and practical experience with a variety of vehicles had taught me how to get optimum performance from an engine, but there wasn't enough room to get the good running start at the hill I needed to gain momentum. It was plain that both vehicle and driver would again be put to the test.

I was accustomed to facing difficulties and solving them with natural understanding and human abilities. Although God had already intervened twice to rescue me on this trip, habit patterns are strong. This new obstacle was approached in the usual way, depending upon the horsepower of the engine and my ability as a driver. I had asked God's protection for the journey, and if I really couldn't handle the situation, he would be available to help me out after I got into trouble. My basic communication was not, "Lord, please take and keep control," but "God, please help *me* to do it." At that time in my life, I was still looking to him for help only when I couldn't handle a situation myself.

About half way up the incline, I realized that this must be the formidable giant the logging driver had warned me about. The glare of the setting sun obscured my sight. The engine was beginning to sound as if it might not be powerful enough for the hill. The memory of hanging over the canyon precipice a few hours before was still vivid in my mind. There was no possibility at that point of backing down this twisted hill with my heavy load. If the motor failed, I would be plunged into the fearful dilemma of "go forward, or lose everything." This time, I sensed no human hand would be near to help. Again, natural resources were failing and again, "This poor man cried." But it was not the call of assured confidence and reliance upon the Lord who sought complete control of my life. It was again a cry of panic and desperation.

Like the Israelites in the wilderness, I was seeing divine intervention over and over again, and like them, my faith continued to fail in a crisis. I had not yet learned to depend on him except as a last resort. With the appearance of each threatening giant, I was conditioned as the Israelites to believe the evil report, "We cannot go in and possess the land."

I knew I could not go back down the hill. I had to keep going or I would lose everything I owned.

As I prayed, "God, help me!" it was if an unseen hand took over driving the car. I imagined myself steering across a level field on my old farm. The engine was revved up, and I began to climb the steep trail like a mountain goat. For an instant, the engine lost power and nearly stalled, even though the accelerator was pressed to the floorboard. Again panic seized me and I almost froze. Something told me I had better hang on and keep praying.

Quickly, the engine seemed to regain its momentum, and with my eyes glued to the increasingly steep road, I dared not stop praying until after the summit was reached. When I got there I had to rest. My legs had turned to rubber. While I could feel the blood pulsing through my veins, I wondered how that six-cylinder engine could have carried my car and trailer up such a steep, winding mountain road. Another verse came to mind: "Not by might, nor by power, but by my spirit, saith the Lord of hosts" (Zech. 4:6).

This trip was taxing my young physical endurance to the limit. I could see that graduation from the school of theology did little more than prepare me to enroll in the school of God's discipline, where the schoolmaster would drive me to Christ.

All the rest of the trip to Prince Rupert seemed downhill. But it taught my young faith and body that there was much to learn about entering into God's rest. I thought often of the meaning of the verse: "Come unto me, all ye that labour and are heavy laden, and I will give you rest" (Matt. 11:28). Until this principle of resting in God could rule every phase of my life and ministry, I would never experience all that God had for me.

GOD GAVE REST

Learning how to rest in God was a long process, which began in a new way on that treacherous road to Prince Rupert. The Lord used other means as well to advance these truths in my life. One important lesson was learned as I was one day meditating upon the creation story in the first two chapters of Genesis.

The biblical account of creation had always fascinated me, but I didn't think it could contain anything that I had not already studied many times before in college. I could recite from memory the events that marked each day of creation.

I noticed again that the first day of creation was marked off by an evening and a morning. Of the second day, Genesis reads, "And the evening and the morning were the second day." All six days of creation were given specific boundaries, marked off by "the evening and the morning." Each of the six days of God's active creation had a beginning, and each had an ending. The sixth day ended with the creation of Adam and Eve, who were given dominion over all else that God had created on earth. God looked at his finished work, was pleased with what he saw, and pronounced it very good.

My attention was then drawn to the next day which had a beginning but of which no ending was mentioned. Unlike the others, it wasn't recorded, "And the evening and the morning were the seventh day." I wondered if it was because on the seventh day God began something which did not end with the closing of that day. I read on.

The day following the sixth must have been the same length as the others. From the fact that it was designated by God as a special day of rest, I concluded that he must have instituted a spiritual reality quite apart and separate from time itself. He established a Rest, or an environment of total peace and security, in which man was to enjoy a never-ending experience of Rest, or trust in God.

"And God blessed the seventh day, and sanctified it: because that in it he had rested from all his work which God created and made" (Gen. 2:3). The Sabbath which God gave to Adam and Eve would continue as long as they continued to rest in God's finished work. They continued in his rest until they allowed human reasoning to replace reliance on God and obedience to him. By shifting their concern from the tree of life to the tree of knowledge, they ceased resting in God's total provision. The first Sabbath ended when Adam and Eve committed the first sin.

I read Genesis chapters one and two again to see if this

interpretation was consistent with other truths I knew about the Bible, especially since I had never heard anyone explain these passages in this manner. The whole creation story took on a different significance for me.

God gave Adam and Eve everything they needed in the Garden of Eden—food, clothing, shelter, health, emotional security, peace, mental stability. So long as they remained true to God, they would never have to work to provide for themselves beyond their responsibilities as stewards of the Garden. There was no need to till the soil. Nothing needed fixing or improving, because the work was done and it was declared by God to be good. The command that man was to work six days and rest on the seventh day was not given to Adam in the Garden of Eden but to Moses on Mt. Sinai. It appears that man's work didn't really begin until after Adam and Eve were expelled from the Garden.

The moment Adam and Eve performed what could be called the first act of "their own works" they lost their Edenic Rest or Sabbath. By turning to his own works, man desecrated that Sabbath and brought it to an end. Scripture records God's pronouncement:

> "And to Adam He said, Because you have listened and given heed to the voice of your wife, and have eaten of the tree of which I commanded you, saying, You shall not eat of it, the ground is under a curse because of you; in sorrow and toil shall you eat [of the fruits] of it all the days of your life; thorns also and thistles shall it bring forth to you; and you shall eat the plants of the field. In the sweat of your face shall you eat bread until you return to the ground, for out of it you were taken; from dust you are, and to dust you shall return. [Gen. 3:17-19, Amp.]

Children are often taught that after God finished the work of creation on the sixth day of the week, he told Adam to rest for twenty-four hours and then go to work, dressing and keeping the garden. But since Adam did not have to provide for his own living nor for any of God's creatures, there was none of that kind of work to do.

We don't really know the full nature of God's original Sabbath. When God made Adam the ruler over his creation, there is nothing to indicate that Adam administered his task in Eden for just six days each week. We don't know if provision was made for Adam to turn his responsibilities over to someone else the seventh day or if the creation was entirely self-sustaining. Since Eden was his home, it appears Adam was responsible for everything that happened there seven days of each week. There was no "preparation day" needed as was the case later among the Israelites, because God himself was the preparation and the provision that all his creation rested and trusted in continuously.

Acts of helpfulness and ministry which were Adam's privilege in Eden were always compatible with true Sabbath keeping, and that was the only kind of activity possible for Adam until the day he sinned. Before the entrance of sin, every day provided a new demonstration of God's perfect provision and was an extension of the complete Rest which God created for man's enjoyment. Jesus said that the Sabbath was made for man, not man for the Sabbath (Mark 2:27).

It is exciting to realize that God gave to man the Sabbath Rest as evidence of his limitless love. Just as man was created for God's pleasure so, Jesus said, the Sabbath was created for man's benefit.

When Eve became dissatisfied with God's work of creation, and thought to add to it by her own works, she was no longer resting and trusting in God's provision. She was seeking to improve on what God had done. To God's perfect works, she added works of her own.

So God explained to Adam that his food and other provisions would no longer be provided as it was for the birds and animals. From that point on, Adam would have to work to provide for himself.

There is a question as to whether the Sabbath of the ten commandments is the same as the Sabbath God gave to Adam in the garden of Eden. The wording indicates that the

Sabbath commandment in its Mosaic form could not have had much significance before Adam sinned.

But when Adam sinned, God pronounced a sentence: "Six days shalt thou labour and do all thy work." This command to labor on his own behalf was the sentence that replaced the Eden Rest, and was the result of sin. Thus, in the heart of the decalogue, right in the middle of the Sabbath commandment, God placed a reminder of the curse of sin to keep before man the memory of the perfect rest which he lost when he chose to walk in his own ways.

The Sabbath commandment contains God's name, his authority, and his dominion. But in addition to these, it also speaks of: (1) God's perfect creation, (2) the permanent Rest God created for man, (3) man's sin, (4) the curse of sin, and (5) the loss of the Rest, full and complete, that God had given to Adam.

The whole story of man's original sin is summarized in the Sabbath commandment, and is contrasted with God's Rest which he gave to Adam.

The Edenic Sabbath and the Mosaic Sabbath are two different things. One was the result of God's perfect creation. The second was a reminder to Israel of the fall of man, and the curse that God put on Adam as a result. Man chose to work, and as a result, God locked him into a life of labor until he should repent and turn away from his own works and again be happy to rest in God's perfect work.

God's original Sabbath was to be a continuous experience. The Mosaic Sabbath came only once in seven days. As the seventh day ended, and the people had to face another week of work, they longed for and prayed for the promised Messiah, who would die to forgive them fully and restore them again to the Edenic state that man had lost.

THE SABBATH RESTORED

When men claim to enter into God's rest every seventh day, they are admitting that they are not experiencing that Rest during the remainder of the week. God calls us to enter into the "full and complete Sabbath rest reserved for the true people of God" (Heb. 4:9, Amp.).

The blessings and warnings God communicates to his people living in these closing days of earth's history are summarized in the angels' messages of Revelation 14:6-11. The first angel's message is a clear call to "worship him that made heaven, and earth, and the sea, and the fountains of waters." This passage directs us to return to the true worship of the Creator who gave to Adam and Eve his perfect Sabbath Rest. By not abiding in God's continuous Sabbath, which began on the seventh day of creation, our first parents ceased to recognize God as truly the creator of all things needed for life. This call is not to return to the Mosaic Sabbath, but to the Sabbath of creation, which provided a rest "full and complete" according to Hebrews chapter four.

Only by accepting the death and resurrection of Jesus as sufficient to redeem us can we again worship God as Creator. Either we accept the righteousness of Jesus as sufficient or we are in as deep trouble as were the Jews who, while observing the Jewish Sabbath, failed to enter into God's Rest. God does not redeem us from the curse contained in the Mosaic Sabbath commandment only to put us back into bondage to that same law again, as Galatians chapter three shows very clearly:

> O you poor *and* silly *and* thoughtless *and* unreflecting *and* senseless Galatians! Who has fascinated *or* bewitched *or* cast a spell over you, unto whom—right before your very eyes—Jesus Christ, the Messiah, was openly *and* graphically set forth *and* portrayed as crucified? Let me ask you this one question: Did you receive the (Holy) Spirit as the result of obeying the Law *and* doing its works, or was it by hearing [the message of the Gospel] and believing [it]?—Was it from observing a law of rituals or from a message of faith? Are you so foolish *and* senseless *and* so silly? Having begun [your new life spiritually] with the

> (Holy) Spirit, are you now reaching perfection [by dependence] on the flesh? Have you suffered so many things *and* experienced so much all for nothing—to no purpose? if it really is to no purpose *and* in vain . . . [Gal. 3:1-4]

After Jesus gave his life to win back what was lost by Adam, and to restore to us his perfect Rest, it would be most ungrateful of us, because of unbelief, to continue to live in the partial rest God gave Israel. We should accept the Rest he bought for us at such a high price. It is his gift to us. We should enter into it.

2
Called to Rest

Recently, I had to go to a distant city to register a new residential lot we owned. It was quite imperative that the registration be done quickly. Other business matters hinged on that registration, and it seemed to us that we needed a miracle. Registration usually takes about two weeks for processing, but we needed it done by the next day.

Taking all the necessary documents we thought we needed, Dorothy and I drove about one hundred miles to the Land Registry office, arriving about nine-thirty in the morning. We were met at the reception desk by a man who checked all the papers and said everything was in order except for a copy of the original land title. Somehow we had failed to bring it along. I explained that the title was in the bank of our hometown one hundred miles away. The agent was polite, but insisted we had to have the missing document.

"How long are you open in the afternoon?" I asked.

"We close at three o'clock," he replied.

"That will give me just enough time to dash back and get it before you close," I said.

"Today? Aren't you angry to have to do all that driving back and forth?" he questioned.

"Not really. Everything will work out just fine," I assured him.

Bug-eyed and openmouthed, he stared at me, then asked, "How can you be so calm and collected? If that were me, I'd be upset. Oh well, I guess there are two kinds of temperaments—you have one and I have the other."

Little did he know how pleased Dorothy and I both were. We realized that, instead of feeling pressured, we felt joyful enough to sing all the way back home. We knew that it was God who was giving us such victory over circumstances. We did not understand why he was requiring the extra trip, but we thanked him for being in charge.

About two that afternoon, we were back in the office with the required document. The secretary who met us checked it over and dismissed us with the assurance that we would hear from them in about two weeks.

"May we complete the registration today?" I asked.

"No, that is not possible. There are many applications for new registrations before yours, and you'll have to wait your turn."

"This is your problem, Lord," I said quietly. "We choose to rest and watch you work it out."

"Who was the gentleman that served us this morning?" I asked the secretary at the counter.

"I can call him if you wish," she responded.

In a few minutes he arrived, smiling and expressing surprise that we had actually returned. Quietly he picked up the papers and completed the registration right there. What normally would have taken two weeks God did in one day.

This is typical of how God works when we allow him to be Lord. If we had brought all the documents the first trip, the registration would have taken two weeks. If I had become upset on discovering that an additional two hundred miles driving would be required, the agent would not have been so willing to bend the rules on our behalf. Our testimony of peace and joy so disarmed him that he processed our documents without delay.

What happened that day witnessed once more that it is possible to have the peace of God which passes understanding. We were enjoying God's Sabbath Rest all that Wednesday as he flooded our hearts with peace.

As it usually happens when God is in charge, we did not know what the results were to be until the last minute. How many times we experience trials but witness no positive results because we destroy the intended blessing with our complaining, our self-pity, or even outright anger and frustration! This lesson Israel had to learn over and over.

ISRAEL'S REST

When God took the Israelites out of Egypt, his original plan was to lead them into Canaan, a situation reminiscent of the Garden of Eden. God did not intend for them to fight their own battles, or to make their own provision during the journey. God promised to control the elements on their behalf, and even to immunize them against sickness if they would but trust him and do all that he asked them to do without grumbling or complaining.

As they began their march out of Egypt, these children of Abraham did not have to lift a sword against the enemy. God defeated the Egyptian armies at the Red Sea with no help at all from Israel. All God required of them was to trust him, march when he gave the orders, and stop when he called a halt. Israel saw for the first time that "it is not by might, nor by power, but by my Spirit, saith the Lord."

There is a carnal way to live and there is a spiritual way to live. God planned to lead Israel into an experience of complete trust in him for all their needs, much as he had provided for Adam.

After crossing the Red Sea, God arranged circumstances so he could give Israel another example of his love and provision. He led them to a desert where there was no water. After three days, when their water supply was running low, they found water from a natural source. But the water was bitter and not fit for human consumption. God had planned to create plenty of good fresh water for them in a place where there was no water in order to convince them that they could always trust him to quench their thirst. They were not to trust their own efforts but the divine source to provide for all their needs.

Unfortunately, Israel turned against God by their grumbling and criticism of the man who had been selected to lead them. In mercy God overlooked their lack of trust and told Moses how to sweeten the water. The healing of the waters at Mara was to be an example of God's desire to heal them of the bitterness resulting from their life of captivity in Egypt, which was poisoning their souls.

After miraculously supplying Israel with water, God further surprised them by providing manna from heaven. Surely Israel would now be convinced that God was able to supply all their needs!

Then to test them, God again caused the water supply to fail. He was giving them another opportunity to trust him and to receive further proof that he not only could, but would, supply all their needs, whatever the circumstances. True to pattern, they again failed to await his provision. God told Moses to speak to the rock. In anger Moses failed also when he struck the rock instead; but plenty of water flowed to satisfy them and their cattle in spite of Moses' anger. But Israel never learned. Instead of trusting God to uphold them by his miracle-working power, they continued to criticize Moses every time they had difficulty understanding what God was doing. Because of their unbelief God wasn't going to give them the Rest he had planned (Heb. 3:17-19).

Since they insisted on viewing things from a natural, or carnal, point of view, God could not reestablish the Abrahamic covenant of faith with them. Consequently, God instituted a covenant based on law until they could learn that "man shall not live by bread alone, but by every word that proceedeth out of the mouth of God" (Deut. 8:3). Israel was allowed about 1500 years, from Moses until the coming of the Messiah, to learn that man's relationship to God is to be one of pure faith untainted by the work of man's hands.

Unfortunately, Israel seemed unable to grasp that lesson and preferred to be governed by their own wisdom, which in turn was based on their previous experiences in the natural world. Their intentions may have been good when they told Moses that "all that the Lord hath spoken, we will do," but that statement revealed the pride and independence that is typical of the natural man.

God told Israel how he planned to give Canaan into their hands (Exodus 23:27-29). God did not plan for them to fight in their own strength and power. He promised to drive the enemy out himself. He did not take them out of Egyptian slavery to confront them with new battles and frustrations but to give them Rest. But they refused to believe that God could defeat the Canaanites, so Israel turned away in unbelief.

God took Israel into the desert where there was nothing to eat so he could show them that he could be their source of food. Instead of trusting that God, who defeated the Egyptians, and who gave them water, could also satisfy their hunger, they began to complain that God had taken them into the desert to kill them. In spite of their attitude, God provided manna. But they continued in stubbornness and rebellion until they locked themselves outside that total peace and rest God wished them to enjoy. They were rejected because of their failure to trust God, and to rest in his perfect provision.

> And to whom did He swear that they should not enter His rest, but to those who disobeyed—who had not listened to His word, and who refused to be compliant or be persuaded? So we see that they were not able to enter [into His rest] because of their unwillingness to

> adhere to *and* trust *and* rely on God—unbelief had shut them out." [Heb. 3:18, 19, Amp.]

The reason Israel later engaged in so many bloodbaths and created a history of such carnage and brutality is because they had rejected God's original plan and insisted on doing their own thing in their own way. They failed to understand that their real enemies were not the Canaanites or the Philistines but the sin of self-sufficiency that lurked in their own hearts. The principle of Revelation 13:10 was fulfilled in Israel. Pride and self-reliance were the giants that closed the doors to Canaan and caused Israel to die in the wilderness outside the Promised Land.

God's call to Israel to leave Egypt and to possess Canaan was a call to turn away from the works of man's hands and trust by faith in the finished works of God. The Lord longed to give them his Rest which was total, full, and complete. It was so all-inclusive that the Israelites did not believe it was possible and rejected it.

This call to experience the Sabbath Rest more fully runs like a golden thread through all the teachings of the New Testament. As Hebrews 4:11 warns us, many today are unwittingly following in the steps of the ancient Israelites: "Let us labor therefore to enter into that rest, lest any man fall after the same example of unbelief."

The Red Sea crossing and the march through the wilderness was a picture of what happens to every Christian when he, by faith, begins to enter God's provision and cease from his own efforts to deliver himself. It is a picture of the salvation experience, the new birth, which takes place when we realize our own work is inadequate and that we must accept God's work on our behalf. Entering into God's Rest is the new beginning—the new birth, as described elsewhere in Scripture.

THE NEW BEGINNING

What is the new birth? Does it have to do only with the mind, or is it more basic than that? I've sometimes heard that God cannot communicate with us except through our understanding. That may be the usual way, but it is not the only way. Does the new birth consist merely in changing one's mind to accept a new set of theories or does it include something more basic—a new life or a new creation?

Is this new birth real or imaginary, literal or figurative, and if real and literal, to what extent? The answer to these questions comes in examining the birth of Christ in the Scriptures.

In Luke 1:35 we read how the angel told Mary that the Holy Spirit would come upon her, and that the power of God would overshadow her for the purpose that a new life be formed within her. That new life was the body which God was preparing to house the preexistent Son of God. In much the same way, the new birth is the beginning of a new life within us.

Probably the clearest account of the nature of the new birth found in the Scriptures is recorded in John 3:1-8. Nicodemus came to Jesus by night because of an emptiness that only God could fill, as is true of each person who has not been made alive by the Holy Spirit. Nicodemus wanted this spiritual fulfillment even though mentally he knew a lot about the Word of God. His knowledge was all in his brain. Although he knew Jesus as an acquaintance, he was not yet born again. The thief on the cross achieved eternal life even though in complete ignorance of many eternal truths. How then, is a man born again?

> Jesus declared, "I tell you the truth, unless a man is born again, he cannot see the kingdom of God." "But," said Nicodemus, "how can a man be born when he is old? Surely he cannot enter a second time into his mother's womb to be born." Jesus answered, "I tell you the truth, unless a man is born of water and the Spirit, he cannot enter the kingdom of heaven. Flesh gives birth of flesh, but the Spirit gives birth to spirit." [John 3:3-6, NIV]

Jesus seemed quite emphatic that the new birth was a real experience—as real as a physical birth, but yet on a different plane, something spiritual apart from physical phenomena. What is born of flesh remains physical, Jesus said, while that which is born of the Spirit (Holy Spirit) is spirit (human spirit). He seemed to indicate that when a man is born again, a new life is formed within him. God's Spirit overshadows the one who comes to Jesus, and enlivens, or more correctly, fertilizes the dormant human spirit which lies "dead" in trespasses and sins in our inner being. The New Testament describes it several ways: "And you hath he quickened, who were dead in trespasses and sins" (Eph. 2:1). "And you, being dead in your sins . . . hath he quickened together with him, having forgiven you all trespasses" (Col. 2:13).

Just as the Holy Spirit touched and fertilized the egg or ovum in the womb of Mary, thus creating a body for the Son of God to dwell in, so also the Holy Spirit is sent to us to fertilize or enliven the dormant or "dead" spirit which was ours when we came into the world. Peter wrote: "You have been regenerated—born again—not from a mortal origin (seed, sperm) but from one that is immortal by the *ever* living and lasting Word of God" (1 Pet. 1:23, Amp.).

The Apostle John explained this mystery further. "No one born (begotten) of God [deliberately and knowingly] habitually practices sin, for God's nature abides in him—His principle of life, the divine sperm, remains permanently within him—and he cannot practice sinning because he is born (begotten) of God" (1 John 3:9, Amp.).

It appears that in the case of Jesus, the spiritual reality existed first and later God prepared for him a body to house the preexistent One who dwelt among us. In our case, we are born first as physical beings, then, by the action of the Holy Spirit upon us, our spiritual natures are brought to life to abide within these mortal bodies.

Just as the Son of God tabernacled among men in a human body, so also our born-again spirit, when brought to life by the contact of the Holy Spirit, tabernacles or dwells in this earthly body.

When we receive God's gift of salvation and leave "Egypt," we, like the Israelites, cross our own Red Sea by faith. But just as they continued to carry their own burdens, and to fight many of their own battles, thus bringing upon themselves defeat after defeat, so many today are trying to accomplish in their own strength that which God says can be accomplished only by him.

How many truly restful Christians do we find today who are experiencing the Rest—full and complete—that Jesus offers? How many know God's total Rest, which promises to remove all anxieties and problems that afflict so many of us? How many today think of salvation and the life of Rest as a pie-in-the-sky unachievable goal? When God removed Israel from Egypt, he offered them relief that was meant to encompass their total physical experience. But because they failed to trust God, they settled for a situation in which they became prisoners under Adam's curse for six days of every week with only one day of reprieve or rest.

Israel failed to keep even the one-day-a-week Sabbath holy, not so much by overt actions as by their inner attitude. Their self-reliance—the attitude, "if we do our best, then God will make up the difference," is the sin that insulated them from God's total provision.

Today, by our attitudes we show the same self-reliance and lack of trust in God. We so easily forget that Christ's robe of righteousness, which God provides for us, contains not one thread of human devising.

REMEMBERING THE SABBATH

As a result of their rebellion and unbelief (Heb. 3:18), they would be permitted to enter into his Rest only one day in seven. He had originally intended that they continuously enjoy his provision in its fullness.

If Adam had not sinned against God, he would not have been sentenced to earn his bread by the sweat of his face. Similarly, if Israel had not sinned by rebellion against God's provision, they would not have been sentenced to a life of hard labor for six days of every week. God could have returned them to Egypt where they probably labored seven days a week, but in mercy, he gave them a commandment to consider the seventh day of every week holy. He commanded them to use that day to reflect on the original creation, and the perfect Rest he gave to Adam and Eve. By doing that, they were also forced to meditate on the Rest they forfeited by their own rebellion and rejection of God's provision for them.

What was Israel to remember about the Sabbath? They were to remember and think about the Edenic experience of total rest, when man trusted in God's complete provision for seven days of every week. They were to remember that God created the heavens and the earth in six days and then rested the seventh day because there was no more work to be done. Included in the fourth commandment were reminders of:

1. God's perfect creation and cessation from work.
2. God's perfect rest that he made for man.
3. The sin that broke the original Sabbath Rest.
4. The fact that they were not presently experiencing the Sabbath Rest God had *begun* on the seventh day of creation week.
5. Israel was to remember the promise of Genesis 3:15, which pointed them to the cross. In that prophecy, God promised to send his Son to die for the sins of men and to restore us again to our Rest in the Lord. The Sabbath commandment would be fulfilled at the cross when the seed of the woman would crush the serpent's head, again making available to man the Rest he had lost.

So the sentence pronounced on Adam's sin is indelibly inscribed by the finger of God in the heart of the Sabbath commandment. It is a constant reminder that the Rest offered in the law given to Moses is at best a partial rest, a breathing spell, a reprieve. God's real Rest was the kind offered by Jesus when he said, "Come unto me, all ye that labor and are heavy laden and I will give you rest" (Matt. 11:28).

That kind of rest is quite a contrast to the commandment where Israel was told: "Six days shalt thou labor and do all thy work." It is no wonder that those who made the Mosaic law their guiding principle, and interpreted it according to the letter of the law, accused Christ of teaching contrary to the law of Moses and crucified him. It is in this very point that we have been warned that we are in danger of repeating the history of Israel and rejecting Christ's gift to us.

How one enters today into this experience of total rest and dependence on God is the next question, and one that must be dealt with separately. Consider some of God's promises to us.

Ephesians 2:8, 9 tells us we are saved by faith, and that it is not by works lest any man should boast. Is this a salvation only from sin itself, or from the results and curse of sin as well? In other words, did God promise Adam and Eve, and later Israel, that he would care for their spiritual welfare and future life only, or did he mean to care for the whole person in every area of living in the present life also? Does Jesus really mean to care for all our temporal needs now? I believe he does.

Jesus said, "Seek ye first the kingdom of God, and his righteousness, and all these things shall be added unto you" (Matt. 6:33). The "all these things" were food, drink, the care of our bodies, and our raiment, as he described in verses twenty-five through thirty-two.

Some people in recent years have read these promises of Jesus, and by their own decision, quit their jobs, and even left their families stranded as they went out to "seek the kingdom of God." Such carnal efforts result in spiritual and physical loss to the Church. Certainly this is not what Christ intended people to do. One cannot enter into God's true Rest by just deciding on his own to do so. The decision must be to seek the Blesser rather than the blessing. As one looks to Jesus, and trusts him to guide, and is willing to be disciplined and matured through trials and hardships, Jesus will give his Rest.

God can give us his Rest in whatever vocation he places us. As we seek to move from the physical bondage caused by sin toward the spiritual Rest promised by Jesus, we should not assume that we can just decide on our own to totally ignore the needs of this life.

Abraham enjoyed God's Rest, yet he had possessions and recognized his responsibility to his family and servants. Joseph as ruler of Egypt enjoyed God's Rest, yet he ruled a kingdom as God directed him. Elisha's case, on the other hand, was different. He literally gave up his occupation when he sacrificed his oxen and burned his plow when God called him, but he stayed busy in God's work the rest of his life.

In all his callings, God requires that we honor our prior commitments, and wait for his guidance in dealing with them. God does not need us, in the sense that he would be helpless without us, but we should rejoice that he chooses to use us.

CHRIST'S REST

The Sabbath experience, which God has reserved for his people, is the theme of Christ's instructions to his disciples as recorded in the Gospel of John, chapters fourteen through seventeen. One of the central themes of Christ's ministry is found in John 16:33: "These things I have spoken unto you, that in me ye might have peace. In the world ye shall have tribulation; but be of good cheer; I have overcome the world."

Then in John 14:27, Jesus said: "Peace I leave with you, my peace I give unto you: not as the world giveth, give I unto you. Let not your heart be troubled, neither let it be afraid."

To understand how to appreciate this peace that Jesus made available to us, we must look into Jesus' life. How did he enter into, and abide in the Rest of his Father? How did God's Sabbath relate to the trials, and temptations, and buffeting by which he was besieged all through his life?

Peter summarized Christ's life this way:

> For Christ suffered for you and left you a personal example, so that you might follow in his footsteps. He was guilty of no sin nor of the slightest prevarication. Yet when he was insulted he offered no insult in return. When he suffered he made no threats of revenge. He simply committed his cause to the One who judges fairly. And he personally bore our sins in his own body on the cross, so that we might be dead to sin and alive to all that is good. [1 Pet. 2:21-24, Phillips]

In this particular text, the term "dead to sin" describes the key by which one may enter into the peace that Jesus offers to us. The above Scripture makes plain that when someone sinned against Jesus, that sinful act did not arouse a negative response in him.

When the Jewish leaders insulted him, he did not return in kind. When he was slandered, he did not even get upset, much less slander in return. When his own people returned evil for good, he felt sorrow and pity for them.

This text in 1 Peter, which says we should be dead to sin, is not speaking only of our ceasing to commit sin against someone else but that we can also become dead to the sins others may commit against us.

It is not easy for the carnal man to obey when Jesus calls: "Come unto me all ye that labor and are heavy laden, and I will give you rest." We want the Rest, but are often unwilling to pay the price of dying to sin. We hate to give up the luxuries of self-defense and self-pity, and so bind ourselves under the curse of sin which isolates us from the peace Jesus offers. There is no substitute for Jesus, the Prince of Peace, enthroned in the heart of the believer.

3
Seeking Rest

Once during the early years of our ministry in the village of Port Edward near Prince Rupert, I arrived at the home of an Indian friend. A little girl told me that her parents, the people I was coming to see, were down at the docks where the fishing boats came in.

I soon located the boat I was looking for only to learn that my friends were in the midst of an emergency. The itinerant Pentecostal minister had had an accident. There in the cabin of the boat I saw lying in the bed the form of the pastor. While traveling up the river, he was overcome by carbon monoxide fumes from a faulty exhaust system. After docking, he had collapsed on the floor and was found by people who came to meet him. All the people in the boat had been gathered around him praying until they turned and saw me entering.

"Here is our Seventh-day Adventist brother. Let him pray that God will restore the pastor!"

I was jolted. "Oh, God," I said, "what do I do now?"

Until that time I had fellowshipped with people who

theoretically knew that God could do miracles and even heal people, but I had actually seen so few results from that kind of intercessory prayer that I had become quite accustomed to praying for miracles without really expecting anything to happen.

Now I was in the midst of just such a crisis. The people who had gathered in the boat were praying people. They knew that God could and would answer prayer. Even though they weren't getting any results, their faith seemed stronger than mine. As they prayed, believing, the pastor still remained near death. Why did they seem to latch onto me, as if expecting more out of my faith and prayers to bring results than they did their own? Because I was a pastor, they thought that I should know more about getting results from God than they did.

I didn't mind joining the group and uniting my prayers to theirs, but I did not know how to place this kind of crisis in the hands of God and enter into his Rest. Past experience had given me secret doubts that this kind of prayer for instant healing would be answered.

I was scared! How had I gotten myself into this? Yet there the pastor was, my friend, near death, and with no doctor close enough to lean on for help. I had to do something—and all I could do was pray.

"God," I cried, "this man needs you now, and I have never seen you heal anyone instantly. Please, God, I need you! Have mercy on us! Please don't let my friend die!"

Forgetting myself and my own feelings of pride and unbelief, I knelt beside the dying man and cried out to God: "Oh, God, please touch my brother, in Jesus' name, Amen." I didn't know what else to say. I was desperate. My concern was not for the pastor alone but for my own impotence in the midst of a crisis.

"Oh, please, God, please, please!" I said quietly. Slowly I opened my eyes, hardly daring to look.

The unconscious man suddenly revived, opened his eyes, and was now looking at us, alert and well. His eyes were clear and alert.

"Glory to God!" I shouted as the whole group joined. We believed that God had healed the man right there before our eyes.

I was aware that skeptical people could find an explanation for what had happened. Perhaps the man needed oxygen to help his system overcome the carbon monoxide poison. As more clean air entered the cabin and his lungs filled with oxygen, the effects of the poisoning were reversed. All that may have been true. But all we knew was that we were beyond ourselves in helping our brother and that when we asked God for the man's recovery, what we were asking of God happened. For us it was God's answer to our prayers in whatever way he wanted to grant it.

For the next few minutes the small cabin glowed as with the presence of Jesus, as the pastor rose up. We all worshiped God with adoration that seemed appropriate to this most intimate touch of the Lord.

The sun had set, and I asked leave to go as I had had a strenuous day and wished to get home. Stepping onto the deck, I realized something was wrong. The boat had been tied to a dock at the mouth of the Skeena River. But there was no dock—only a wide expanse of water. The boat had broken loose and was already in the main current of the mighty Skeena River and was being swept out into the Pacific. A veteran fisherman on board told us all to be calm and he would get us back with no difficulty. He tried to start the engine but it failed to respond. Upon checking the propeller, he found that the main pin was sheared off. The motor was revving, but nothing was happening as the propeller was standing still on the shaft. He searched the boat but there was no replacement pin for the propeller.

As darkness deepened, a strange sort of fear began to make itself felt among us. All fishing boats were normally in before dark, so we faced the prospect of being swept out into the path of ocean-going ships before the next morning. Having just witnessed a miracle, I suggested that we ask God for another one. How soon we forget, I thought. The verse came to my mind: "Come unto me, all ye that labor and are heavy laden, and I will give you rest" (Matt. 11:28).

We bowed our heads and simply asked God for another miracle. It just did not seem to make sense that God would heal a man just to let us all go down the river and into the path of danger. We thought of the verse: "All things work together for good to those who love God." The Lord must have a purpose for this also, we agreed.

Looking out over the dark waters, we soon spotted a small light coming, a boat making its way upriver. To attract his attention, we shouted and waved our arms in the darkening gloom. The fisherman happened to hear us and saw us beckoning him. He had been detained and was going home late, but was just in time to be God's answer to our prayers. It was a happy group that meditated on the goodness of God as we were slowly being towed back to the village and safety.

This experience on the river only intensified my desire to find out why I was usually living so far below my potential as a child of God. If God could meet my needs in a crisis, why not in everyday life? Is God willing to help us keep out of trouble, or does he only come to the rescue after we get ourselves into impossible situations? These were questions to which I felt I just had to find answers. It was not long until I began to learn a bit more of what the Bible meant when it said that one does not build up the kingdom of God by using wood, hay, and stubble—gimmicks and programs (1 Cor. 12).

SEEKING A VITAL RELATIONSHIP

I had, through years of ministerial training, developed many concepts and attitudes which, rather than helping my spiritual life, had insulated me from the vital presence of the Holy Spirit. The glow and warmth I occasionally felt from the nearness of Jesus was priceless. But I often mourned over my lack of a continuing, daily communion with my Lord. Why did prayer seem to work one day, and the next it seemed that my prayers would not get past the ceiling?

Why was my communication with Jesus so sporadic? During the next years, my ministry had the form of godliness but was lacking in power.

Looking back on those years, I recall vividly the weeks of intense preparation that preceded every evangelistic campaign, which ironically we called "efforts."

We used to watch for the latest visual aids available on the market. We tried to obtain the best meeting hall with the most comfortable facilities. We advertised, using the catchiest slogans we could think up, and if there was any gimmick we could use to win souls to Christ, we used it.

Our crusades were based largely on sheer hard work and logic. Then, after we expended our might and our power, we trusted, or rather hoped that the Holy Spirit might make up for any deficiency we might have had or overlooked. It is no wonder we became tired, worn out, and often frustrated. We were not resting in the yoke with Jesus but working as though the salvation of the world depended on our puny efforts. If every ounce of our energy was not burned up, we feared that God would hold us responsible for those lost souls we might have reached if we had worked harder. Practical experience had not yet taught us what Jesus meant when he said: "Take my yoke upon you, and learn of me . . . for my yoke is easy, and my burden is light" (Matt. 11:29, 30).

It was not that I didn't want God's power for ministry as some suggested. I knew I needed the same spiritual vitality that made Peter, John, and Silas such vibrant witnesses to the early church. A desire was growing within me to be filled to overflowing with the water Jesus promised to the woman at the well. As I faced crisis after crisis, God saw me through, but I had a growing realization that God wanted to prepare me for a more vital relationship with himself. I was experiencing an increasing restlessness in my heart. I longed to become more personally acquainted with the Lord, but to me it seemed that I could only progress so far and no farther. My hunger for him continued to deepen, and the pangs were at times so intense that I would cry out for a deeper sense of his presence. I did not know it at the time, but God was making me willing to be stripped of any ideas or concepts that were incompatible with the way the Holy Spirit would work. Dorothy and I often prayed for God to show us what was keeping us merely on an acquaintance level with him. We were no longer satisfied to know all *about* him. We had to find a way to get to know *him* in a more personal way.

While conducting a crusade in Port Alberni on the west coast of Vancouver Island during the winter of that year, matters came to a head for us. Our campaign was planned in detail as usual. All the advertising was in place. The prelecture movies on the life of Christ were beautiful. The incentive prizes for regular attendance were neatly promoted. The various aids and supports were used with maximum effectiveness, and the people were becoming interested in what we had to say. Regular follow-up work kept us very busy, and it was quite evident that we were headed for another "success." Yet, the gnawing hunger for a deeper experience with Jesus kept growing inside of me. I couldn't shake it off. It was not a particularly enjoyable situation at all, but God was busy trying to answer my prayer.

Little did I realize what those years of ministry could have been if only I had known more of what it really meant to enter into the Rest God had prepared for me.

Years later we realized what it was to be in the yoke with Jesus. The story of Charles Finney was a real inspiration to me, and helped teach me how to relate to Jesus in such a way that he could take over and do the work which I used to think was my job.

We were told that before Charles Finney began an evangelistic campaign, rather than struggle as we had with films, advertising slogans, and incentive prizes, he often went out into the woods alone with God, and there wrestled in prayer for the salvation of a town until he literally groaned in the spirit as though suffering birth pangs for the sinners whom God had laid upon his heart. This kind of intercession was described by Paul: "My little children, for whom I am again suffering birth pangs until Christ is completely and permanently formed (molded) within you!" (Gal. 4:19, Amp.).

Then, when Finney was convinced by the Spirit in his heart that the Lord had given him the victory, he would go into the town to find that the Holy Spirit was already at work. Men and women by the score were repenting in the streets and in the factories and turning to God.

Finney was in the yoke with Jesus. His campaign was waged chiefly on his knees before God. Then, after God had broken the power of the enemy through his prayer, he would go into the city to witness what the Lord was already doing. The Holy Spirit had prepared the hearts of the people before Finney stood up to preach. His preaching was simply the means by which God brought to view the work that the Holy Spirit had already done in the hearts of those who were to be saved.

Finney's success was due more to his power in prayer than to his ability as a preacher. He knew that to win victories in spiritual realms he had to rely on spiritual weapons, and that the sword of the Spirit can be wielded far more effectively when the Holy Spirit is a partner in the warfare.

One evening just as I finished speaking before a large crowd, a voice inside me seemed to ask the question: If you were putting this much effort, and this much scheming, and this much baiting into working for any political organization, wouldn't you probably get just as many good results?

The question devastated me. At home that night, I told Dorothy that I was finished with public evangelism until I could find the answer for my lack of spiritual power. I saw that God was not honored by the service we thought we were rendering to him. He wanted not our service—he wanted us! Unless the Holy Spirit could work through us as he did through the apostles, I realized that we were merely offering to God the works of our own hands as did Cain.

I continued pastoring, but spent every morning in prayer and Bible study. Gradually, as the light started to break and I began to see what some of my spiritual hang-ups were, I tried to share my concern and spiritual needs with some of the men of our church conference. I talked to several of the ministers, but found no response. None seemed to share my concern. One man, the pastor of a large church in British Columbia, told me that he could not help because he had no time for personal study. From early morning until late each night, seven days a week, he was so burdened with the problems of administration and numerous church programs that there just weren't any hours left when he could be alone with God. He was so burdened *serving God,* that he had no time *for God.* He had not learned how to find rest in the yoke with Christ. Spiritually, he was a slave, not a son.

One of the questions I asked myself during those days of study was, Am I laboring under the yoke of a schoolmaster? Am I ready to learn from Jesus and exchange the yoke of bondage for his yoke? He said, "Take my yoke upon you, and learn of me . . . For my yoke is easy, and my burden is light" (Matt. 11:29, 30).

How was I to enter into this rest that Jesus offered to me? I wondered. The key to the answer was summarized by Jesus in the next passages.

"Come unto me, all ye that labor and are heavy laden, and *I will give you* rest [italics mine]. Take my yoke upon you, and learn of me; for I am meek and lowly in heart: and *ye shall find* rest unto your souls [italics mine]."

I saw that Jesus offered his rest as two separate experiences. First, he invites us to "come," and if we do, he promises to *give* us rest. This is the Rest which is inherent in salvation and is given freely to all who come. He asks only that we come, and give him our sinful hearts that he may give us new hearts. Upon surrendering the sinful nature which delights in the things of sin and self, Christ gives us new hearts which feel at rest in the presence of God. We are accepted in Christ, and are seated with him in his throne at the Father's right hand. This is the Rest he promises to give us at salvation.

Then the second step is the "finding" of rest which comes as we allow ourselves to be yoked up with him in service. It was here that I had so much to learn. Service didn't necessarily bring rest. Unless entered into according to the leading of the Holy Spirit, it is possible to lose the peace and the sense of joy which even the first rest brings. In such a state, it is difficult for us to come to the second and deeper experience of rest in the yoke.

Before taking up the yoke of service, Paul spent three years in Arabia becoming acquainted with God. After his baptism, Jesus spent forty days in the desert. After he sensed his mission to deliver Israel from Egypt, Moses spent forty years in the desert learning to recognize God's voice. Every person, after he is born again, needs a time to learn to know Jesus personally.

When our souls are spiritually prepared, and God's timing for us is fulfilled, then we will recognize the hand of God gently placing the yoke upon us, and with Jesus, our elder brother, we begin to move as the Spirit leads. We only follow as he directs, and as he leads *he* performs the work. Our privilege is having a part in the work—not doing the work ourselves.

In the yoke, ours is the privilege to walk at Jesus' side to observe and marvel at what he does. Only by *following* as the Spirit leads can we find rest "in" the yoke. As soon as we sense we are losing our rest, we should stop immediately and determine where we are beginning to walk independently of the Holy Spirit. So long as we walk as the Holy Spirit leads, we will continue to find a divine peace which defies description. It is not a rest as the world gives, but a deep abiding experience which can only result from knowing God personally, and abiding in his love.

These were some of the lessons we had not yet learned.

But as we waited and searched the Scriptures, God began to reveal them to us. It brought us to a place of decision.

Continuing to seek the Lord, Dorothy and I sensed that we were at a crossroads. Either we would press on to find a more intimate relationship with the Lord or we would soon get caught up in the world of religious activity which could forever close us out from accomplishing any genuine service to the Lord Jesus.

MAKING CHOICES

The months that followed were filled with revelations of things as they were, in contrast with things as they might be. I learned that even my own church had traditions and customs that had become part of our religious life. Any hint that there might be something more to the Christian experience beyond what the church was officially prepared to recognize, was taken as an affront to the organization. I was reminded that God's government is run by God, and that he makes his wishes known first to the elected and recognized leaders, then through them to the people.

"God rules from top down, not from the bottom up," I was told.

I had no argument with how God leads or rules. All I knew was that I felt God had something more for me, and that I might have to choose between my career as a minister with the church in which I had spent all my life and a burning desire to become personally acquainted with Jesus Christ.

Since that time, I have often noticed that God does not always lead everyone in exactly the same way. Jesus' words to Peter in John 21:22 often comforted me when I saw ministers of different faiths free to grow up in the Spirit, while retaining their ministry to the people. In reply to Peter's question about John's future role, Jesus replied: "What is that to thee? Follow thou me."

I had not yet learned how to rest my total being at Jesus'

feet and find my complete satisfaction in simply trusting him. It troubled me that my superiors counseled me to stay within the boundaries prescribed by the church, to quit asking questions, or else I might find myself fighting against God.

Rather than compromise my faith and my hope for a deeper experience than I had known, I chose to resign my post, which at that time included most of Vancouver Island. One kindly brother asked me how I intended to make a living. I had to face the truth that I had not prepared for any alternative profession and now had nowhere to turn but to the Lord.

"That is mighty poor security for a wife and family," I was reminded. To give up a guaranteed salary and pension plan for some unproved spiritual quest was not the smartest thing a practical person could do by any reasonable human standard.

Dorothy was with me daily in prayer as we sought the Lord for direction. We got only one answer, which was "Choose!" We sensed absolutely no direction at all except that we knew that we were at a fork in the road where we had to choose. And we knew that the choice we made would mark our course for the rest of our lives. So it was that my resignation was tendered and we were free—but free to do what?

I felt led to go back to the cities of Prince Rupert and Terrace to look for work. Practically penniless, we stopped in Terrace where I canvassed every single establishment searching for employment. There was nothing available because business was in recession and unskilled labor was plentiful.

Finally I got a job in construction, moving heavy beams into place by hand in the pouring rain. I remember rushing home for lunch, and while I ate, Dorothy would help me out of my wet clothes and into dry things so I could get back on the job in thirty minutes. This routine continued day after day until she put her foot down.

She said that she needed me more than we needed the money. I was killing myself physically and had no time to spend with her either. I knew I couldn't keep up the pace much longer.

"Lord, what do we do now?" we prayed. Then one day Dorothy asked whether I had applied at the school board office for a teaching position. I hadn't, because there seemed to be no use, I replied. I did not have a teacher's certificate nor any of the required teacher training. But she felt I ought to try. At first I refused. She kept insisting that I apply for a teaching job until I thought it would take less effort to do so than to balk at the idea any longer.

In the school board office I was asked for qualifications. I assured the officer that I was well qualified since I had experience in running youth retreats, in preaching, and I had a bachelor's degree in theology, but most important, I knew I could do the job.

"Where did you get your teaching certificate?" I was asked.

"Well, I don't have one."

"Just how much teacher training did you have?"

"I didn't have any," I replied.

"What makes you think you can teach school?"

"I just know it," I assured him. "Look," I added, "give me a chance for two weeks, and if you aren't pleased, do not pay me."

The next day I returned for the verdict and was overjoyed to learn that I had a job. Since it was the middle of October, there was only one vacancy in the district, and that was in Hazelton, a remote Indian village. I returned home with mixed feelings. We knew that Hazelton was one of the most primitive and isolated villages in British Columbia and we did not exactly relish the idea of taking two young children to live there. But I left the construction job and we moved to Hazelton, and thanked God for providing a job in such an unusual way.

For three years we lived there and God did some deep

work in our lives. There he gave us our first real home. We heard that some old houses were being sold off in Kitimat, about 125 miles away. We bought three of them for five hundred dollars each and spent one summer taking them apart and transporting the usable lumber to Hazelton. It was a hard way to build, but we will never forget the feeling when we moved in late in the fall. It was so good to know it was our own! And we were happy, even though it was nearly another year before we had running water.

More important than the job, the new home, and the other provisions God made for us were the lessons God was teaching us in those days about resting in him.

4 Resting in the Yoke

Shortly after we moved into our new house in Hazelton, we had a most welcomed visitor. Joan was the wife of the Pentecostal pastor—the one whom the Lord had restored after the carbon monoxide poisoning. One day Joan decided to come to see us. She said that she felt God was about to open up our lives to a broader ministry to himself.

One matter was uppermost in our minds, though. We were hungry for more than just an intellectual knowledge of God. We knew there had to be a difference between the service of works like that which Martha gave to Jesus and the more satisfying service of love such as that which Mary offered which Jesus deemed to be better.

Joan and Dorothy and I set aside three days just to seek God and sit at the feet of Jesus. We especially prayed that we might experience a deeper infilling of the Holy Spirit. The three days passed, and at the time we were not particularly aware that any specific change had taken place in us. As we look back now, we can see that the Holy Spirit had begun to work in our lives in a new way.

We still did not have running water in our house at that time. I hauled water in a forty-five-gallon gasoline drum from a nearby spring and then into the house by bucket. As soon as we could afford it, I decided to dig a well. A neighbor asked where I intended to find water.

"In the yard," I replied.

"There is no chance of water on your hillside," he said. "You are situated on a solid rock, and numerous tests have shown that there is no water on your property."

A funny hollow feeling crept through me and into the pit of my stomach. I knew better than to build a house before checking for water. How could I have done such a stupid thing?

As Dorothy and I prayed, we felt, in spite of the neighbor's warning, a strange peace about the situation. I marked out a spot near the house and began to dig. At about three and one-half feet I reached bedrock. The neighbor was right. I took a few days to think the matter through. One night I had a dream in which I dug down through the rock and, at a depth of exactly twelve feet, we found plenty of water. I told Dorothy about the dream the next morning.

I hired a man with a jackhammer to drill into the rock and blast it with dynamite. Each day we went down about eighteen inches. Finally, one morning I looked into the hole and saw that it was nearly half full of water. Overjoyed, I called Dorothy and together we praised God for providing us with water from the solid rock. We could see the precious liquid running in from a crack in the rock on the east side of the hole.

It was several days later before we remembered the details of my dream. We took a tape measure and ran it to the bottom of the well. The mark at the edge of the hole read twelve feet. We realized that God had spoken to us in my dream.

Our water came from "the Rock" in a real sense of the word. The well never ran dry. In fact, the water level stayed at three feet *above* the level of the road which ran about twenty feet away. People shook their heads in amazement as they looked at the height of the water.

We thanked God again and again for beginning to fulfill in our lives his promises which he gave in Isaiah 44:3: "For I will pour water upon him that is thirsty, and floods upon the dry ground: I will pour my spirit upon thy seed, and my blessing upon thine offspring." We took this provision of literal water as a sign of God's answer to prayer concerning spiritual resources as well.

From that moment, God began to fulfill to us other promises from his Word. "And it shall come to pass afterward, that I will pour out my spirit upon all flesh; and your sons and your daughters shall prophesy, your old men shall dream dreams, and your young men shall see visions. And also upon the servants and upon the handmaids in those days will I pour out my spirit" (Joel 2:28, 29). These verses were quoted in Acts 2:16-18 by Peter as the evidence of the arrival of the promised Holy Spirit. In a real sense, we were entering into a fuller experience of the Spirit at work within us.

After my first year as school teacher, I was made principal of the elementary school in New Hazelton, another village four miles away. In this promotion, we saw again how the promises were being fulfilled which Jesus made that if we would seek first his kingdom that all "these things" would be added to us. As we put him first, he would meet our needs. God was truly supplying as he did for Moses in the wilderness—water and manna. The water was from our "miracle" well—the manna was from the "miracle" job.

EXCEPT A CORN OF WHEAT DIE

There were several active churches in the area of Hazelton, and we chose to attend one of the same denomination in which I had ministered. Dorothy and I felt that if we would just show love and if we worked to the best of our abilities to help the church, we would be accepted. But news travels fast, so they were expecting us. For three years we tried to prove ourselves—that we weren't heretics, or disloyal to God or the church. Through resigning from the ministry, I had made myself of no reputation, and it was only natural I suppose that our motives should have been questioned as to why we had given up the ministry and gone into what could be called secular work.

God taught us a very important truth through that experience of feeling unaccepted and our motives being questioned. The truth we learned was that a person cannot prove himself. He cannot clear himself of false accusations because the rumor factory can turn stories out faster than any one person can put them down. We began to understand what the Psalmist had in mind when he wrote: "Cast thy burden upon the Lord, and he shall sustain thee" (Ps. 55:22).

We turned the whole matter of our questionable reputation over to God and chose to trust him. We saw why Jesus did not waste his time trying to vindicate himself. He committed his own reputation into God's hands and sought only to do the will of his Father in heaven.

Job 13:15 took on new meaning for us: "Though he slay me, yet will I trust him." We began to sense that that was exactly what God had in mind for us. We were being readied and prepared for a deeper death to self than we had ever known before. We thought we had surrendered everything to him. We knowingly held back nothing from God. I had given up my career, my ministry, and had gone to the end of the earth, so to speak, for my faith. Yet, we sensed that there was something more to do—God wanted to do a still deeper work in us. We were again being led to a cross experience.

The greatest shock we received came when God allowed us through our studies and prayers to see that all our former religious experience was centered more on doctrines than on the person of Jesus Christ. It was devastating to discover the possibility that some of the things we had been taught as facts in college were not true. The final blow fell when I realized that I could not even depend entirely on my own intelligence, or on the intelligence of others to correctly understand the Word of God, and that the deep truths of God can only be understood as the Spirit reveals them to us and gives the insight. Paul wrote: "For to us God revealed them [spiritual truths] through the Spirit; for the Spirit searches all things, even the depths of God . . . . The natural man does not accept the things of the Spirit of God; for they are foolishness to him, and he cannot understand them, because they are spiritually appraised" (1 Cor. 2:11, 14, NASB). Peter wrote: "But know this first of all, that no prophecy of Scripture is a matter of one's own interpretation, for no prophecy was ever made by an act of human will, but men moved by the Holy Spirit spoke from God" (2 Pet. 1:20, 21, NASB).

We realized for the first time that just as Bible teaching, or prophecy as it is sometimes called, did not originate in the human mind, so likewise, the correct understanding of Bible teaching, or prophecy, could not originate in the human mind. Only as the Holy Spirit chooses to reveal God's mysteries to us can we truly know the will of God. Paul prayed for the Ephesians: "that the God of our Lord Jesus Christ, the Father of glory, may give to you a spirit of wisdom and of revelation in the knowledge of Him. I pray that the eyes of your heart may be enlightened, so that you may know what is the hope of His calling, what are the riches of the glory of His inheritance in the saints" (Eph. 1:17, 18, NASB).

After this realization followed times of complete helplessness. We knew that we could not trust our own intelligence to reveal to us the real truth; yet we were not acquainted with a better way. We certainly did not feel we rated any special consideration from God. We had left all to follow Christ and to find that personal communion with him. He had unquestionably been teaching and discipling us; yet, what of the call to the ministry which had once sounded so clearly within my heart? We cried before the Lord until one day I confessed to Dorothy that I was finished—destroyed.

"I'm completely washed up and of no use to God or anybody. Even my own family doesn't seem to have any confidence in me. I am impotent and incapable of helping even one single soul." I thought she was about to try to soothe my hurt.

Instead she said, "Possibly this is what God was waiting for all the time. Now that you really feel at the end of yourself, maybe God can resurrect you to new life." I thought of the verse: "Verily, verily, I say unto you, except a corn of what fall into the ground and die, it abideth alone: but if it die, it bringeth forth much fruit."

I realized that Dorothy was probably right. I was certain that God didn't want me to stay so discouraged and feeling so useless. I began to think through again all that was involved in entering into God's Rest. How could I analyze my life to see what was missing?

As a result, I set down seven basic steps that I knew from Scripture and from the way the Lord had led me in the past of what was necessary to enter into God's Rest and continue to walk in his provision. I have used these seven foundation steps many times in instructing others in how to enter God's Rest.

HOW MAY I ENTER?

1. The first step certainly is to recognize the invitation that Jesus gave to Nicodemus: "You must be born again" (John 3:7). "Whosoever will may come," Jesus said (Rev. 22:17).

I knew I had taken the first step of recognizing God's call to salvation.

2. The second step was to ask God to give me the new birth. I simply had to believe God would do it; I had to

prove my faith by asking God to do in me what he had promised (John 1:12).

3. Next, I had to accept thankfully what God had done. When I first asked God to give me the new birth, he began that work at the moment I asked him. I may or may not have felt any immediate change, but it was happening anyway. Faith is thanking God for the new life before I see the evidence. It is there because God said so. "Him that cometh to me I will in no wise cast out" (John 6:37).

Scripture further describes it: "Now faith is the assurance of things hoped for, the conviction of things not seen" (Heb. 11:1, NASB). This kind of faith is contrary to human reason and often conflicts with the evidence of the senses. But it has been proven to work! It is almost like creating your own reality by trusting and believing the promises of God. Jesus said, "All things are possible to him that believeth" (Mark 9:23).

4. I had to confess that I was presently receiving the new nature. Acting on the basis of the truth was part of receiving the answer. Unless I truly believed I had received it, it wouldn't have helped anyway. If I do not believe a bridge is strong enough to support me to cross the stream, the bridge might just as well not be there as far as I am concerned. Paul wrote: "If you openly admit by your own lips that Jesus is Lord, and if you believe in your own heart that God raised Him from the dead, you will be saved" (Rom. 10:9, Phillips). Paul said "believe in your heart" and not "believe in your mind." The verse seems to suggest that believing goes far beyond just a mental assent.

5. I had to develop the habit of thanking God every day for the work he was doing in me. Paul wrote: "For I am confident of this very thing, that He who began a good work in you will perfect it until the day of Christ Jesus" (Phil. 1:6, NASB). In another place he wrote: "But thanks be to God, who gives us the victory through our Lord Jesus Christ" (1 Cor. 15:57, NASB).

6. I had to learn to praise God. God will never leave us

nor forsake us, yet experience has shown that all Christians are allowed to pass through times when it seems that God has ceased to be present in their lives—as Dorothy and I were going through at that time. At such times, the Christian feels alone, and heaviness tends to settle upon him. The sure remedy for dispelling the darkness and finding again the light and joy is to begin in the area of the will by praising God for his goodness. Praise is offered—not because the person feels like it, but because God is worthy of it, and further, he commands it. As we obey God and get busy praising him, we experience release in our spirits. Acting in agreement with God's will is not hypocrisy. "Let us offer a constant sacrifice of praise to God—the tribute of our lips which openly acknowledge his name" (Heb. 13:15, Phillips). The Psalmist wrote: "Seven times a day do I praise thee" (Ps. 119:164). There is an immediate reward to those who obey this law and praise God: "Great peace have they which love thy law: and nothing shall offend them" (Ps. 119:165).

Those who tried to find peace by attempting to keep the law on stone have never matured to the place where nothing could offend them. They were always being offended by one another. They were even offended by the Son of God and they crucified him. Such people would likewise be offended by someone trying to call them to rest from their efforts. But those who continue to live in praise to God shall find great peace in their souls.

7. I had to learn the secret which would cause a spiritual child to mature into an adult. The secret is found in Jesus' words to his followers just before his ascension: "I will send forth upon you what my Father has promised; but remain in the city (Jerusalem) until you are clothed with power from on high" (Luke 24:49, Amp.).

All those who are drawn to God are attracted by the Holy Spirit. Those who respond to the call of the Spirit, and are born again, are born of the Spirit as Jesus told Nicodemus. At conversion the Holy Spirit can be placed in control of the mind, and he causes us to want to serve Jesus Christ. But, as

Paul wrote in Romans chapter seven, the inner man, having been programmed by years of negative impulses to reject the call of faith, cannot obey the call of the Spirit through the conscious mind.

Every thought, impression, and experience entering the human mind is stored somewhere in the subconscious. To make decisions and form conclusions, the conscious mind, operating somewhat like a computer, draws upon this stored knowledge and programmed responses.

When a promise of faith recorded in God's Word does not harmonize with what we may have experienced in the natural world, the mind may not be able to relate or respond positively to that promise.

For example, God's Word says, "Casting all your care upon him; for he careth for you" (1 Pet. 5:7). This thought enters my rational, thinking mind. The subconscious may find a conflict between this new impulse and some previous information it has recorded from the natural world, such as "God helps those who help themselves." Because the two statements are contradictory, the new information may be rejected by the subconscious.

Unless I have been born again of the Spirit, my mind has no programming or foundation on which to function. It must be taught to respond in a new, Spirit-directed way until it becomes reprogrammed.

What happens when scriptural truths are fed in and the subconscious rejects them? Frustration. But all is not lost! The new inner man speaks up, as it were: "Let me take over. I can function apart from your natural responses from a new base called faith."

The Spirit of God is able to commune through the Word to the inner man that has been born of the Spirit. "As many as are led by the Spirit of God, they are the sons of God" (Rom. 8:14), Paul explained.

As I allow the inner man to respond, faith begins to grow. As Abram of old was told to go out into a new country, and as he obeyed, even though he did not have a clue where he was going, so I begin to trust. I begin like Peter to take those first unsteady steps of faith upon the water—the sea of my own circumstances. I move out of the natural safety of the boat, which are my natural solutions to problems.

It is possible to program this new experience of faith into the subconscious memory as our minds are being renewed (Rom. 12:2). The next time scriptural truth is heard, the mind receives the new message with more favor. By this operation of faith, the old negative and natural impulses are gradually replaced by the positive behavior based on faith as we allow our minds to be transformed.

The inner harmony that develops, allowing us to believe, is a prerequisite to receiving answers to the prayer of faith. James described this internal wavering within the Christian as a double mind. "For let not that man expect that he will receive anything from the Lord, being a double-minded man, unstable in all his ways" (James 1:7, 8, NASB).

Paul described the same internal struggle within a person: "Wretched man that I am! Who will set me free from the body of this death?" (Rom. 7:24, NASB).

The answer, of course, is in Romans 8:1: "There is therefore now no condemnation for those who are in Christ Jesus." Jesus is the answer. As a remedy to the problem of a war within the soul we are told, as in Ephesians 4:23, that we must have our minds renewed. Second Corinthians 4:16 teaches that the mind must be renewed day by day. This means that it takes time to reprogram our minds so that they will not reject or cancel out the impulses that the Holy Spirit brings.

Abraham seemed to experience the same kind of wavering. One part of him wanted to laugh with Sarah at the news of a son they were to have. Yet Hebrews says that they later believed God, "since she [Sarah] considered him faithful who had promised" (Heb. 11:11).

The Holy Spirit works to deal with our sinful nature to bring it into harmony with God's Word. Our part in the reprogramming is to saturate ourselves with the Word of

God until by constant repetition and reflection on the Word the Holy Spirit has more and more control of us. Paul wrote of the influence of the Scriptures: "having cleansed her [the Church] by the washing of water with the word" (Eph. 5:26).

A double-minded man can receive nothing from God by faith (James 1:7, 8). But as soon as our personality comes under the Spirit's control, we are no longer a house divided against itself. Then we can approach God as a unified personality, believing in our minds and hearts the promises of God. Then, whatever we ask in faith, in harmony with the Word of God, we shall receive (Matt. 21:22).

These were some of the basic lessons the Lord began to show me during that dark waiting period of my life. There were more periods of questioning and impatience with our spiritual growth, but the Lord sent a number of people to us who were very helpful.

Once during that interval, when Dorothy and I were passing through a particularly long and trying experience, we began to wonder all over again about the promises of rest and how they applied to us. We were still working for the Lord as he gave us strength and opportunity, but we certainly were finding no peace or rest. Spiritually we did not know what was wrong. Mentally we were perplexed at all the problems. Physically we were worn out, and our nerves were rather frayed. I was still teaching school at the time, and a variety of activities helped to keep my mind off our spiritual perplexities. Dorothy, however, was at home along with the children and her thoughts. Because she was alone, she perhaps was feeling more of the pressure than I was.

One day while I was away, a car drove into the yard and a kindly lady whom we had met on one other occasion greeted my wife. "God told me to come and see you," she announced.

Miss Whitehead was a retired lady living alone. She had gained an unusual sensitivity to the promptings of the Holy Spirit. That morning, as she prayed, she felt a strong and clear urge in her heart to come out and visit us. As she continued to pray, the urge became stronger and stronger until she felt compelled to obey and said, "All right, Lord, I'll go visit Dorothy today."

She had no car, but she knew from experience that if the call was truly from God, he would provide the transportation. With that in mind, she put on her coat, went to the door, and said, "Thank you, Lord, I know you'll provide a ride for the seventy-mile trip."

In just a few minutes a car stopped at her door and the lady driver asked Miss Whitehead if she wished to go north on Highway 97. She explained that she just felt impressed to stop and inquire. Someone else was sensitive to the Spirit's urging.

"Why yes, I've been expecting you," was the happy reply.

Miss Whitehead stayed with us several days and really said very little about God's leadings except that we felt a deep calm in her soul. Then one morning, unable to sleep and agitated in her mind, Dorothy got up at four A.M. and began to iron the clothes. At nine o'clock, Miss Whitehead arose and asked Dorothy to rest awhile. "I heard you when you awoke," she said. "You are not resting in the Lord." Then she told this story.

IN THE HARNESS WITH JESUS

An ambitious young ox was placed in the harness and allowed to plow a field. All day long he worked as hard as he could, determined to do as much as possible for the master. At nightfall when he retired, the master looked out and saw the field criss-crossed in all directions with furrows. The field was plowed, all right, but what a mess! Any farmer knows that unless the furrows are drawn according to a suitable pattern, the ground is not properly cultivated. Many weeds are missed and will continue to grow. All that effort is wasted.

Next day the master placed the same ox in a yoke beside

a trained ox. This time the older ox took the lead and the furrows were straight. Every inch of ground was properly turned. The field was plowed in less time, with less effort, and with much greater satisfaction to the master. This time the young ox, in addition to pulling, was following the trained ox. He merely walked at the side of the experienced one, but in the end also received approval, not because of what he did, but because he was willing to be led and taught. In following and trusting the older ox, he had experienced a relatively pleasant day, but then also received recognition for a job well done.

"You are just like the young ox," Miss Whitehead said. "Jesus wants you to yoke up with him. He will show you how to pull the load and he will be beside you to help with the task. He will carry your burdens. Your purpose in the yoke is not just to work for God, but that you might have fellowship with Jesus as he works, that you may share in his reward. Jesus does not need your efforts," she emphasized, "he wants you to rest and enjoy his fellowship."

"If you do not find rest while working with Jesus, it is very likely that you are on the wrong side of the yoke," she explained. "Jesus' yoke is made in such a way that the load is pulled by the one who is on the side intended for him. When he is in his place, and you in yours, then your work is easy. When he is left out of the picture, you will fail."

Dorothy and I will not forget the lesson Miss Whitehead came to teach us. Doing God's work means doing it as we are properly yoked with Jesus. Then the work is done correctly—the furrows are straight, and the acceptance of our work by God is sure.

5
Rest Beyond the Veil

As Dorothy and I continued our studies in the Word, we realized that some of the doctrines we had formerly accepted raised many questions about the Christian's relationship to the Old Testament law. What then was the purpose of the law? we wondered.

As I was considering this question, I thought of something that had happened to me when I was a boy. The rolling hills of southern Saskatchewan provided me, as I was growing up, with many exciting experiences I shall never forget. One late afternoon in November, I walked about three miles to a distant pasture to bring the horses home. I chose to walk so that I could set weasel traps in some stone piles along the way. Several fences separated the various fields and pastures, so I crawled through the barbed wire from field to field.

At dusk it began to snow lightly, but that did not concern me at the time. I knew the countryside like the back of my hand. After setting the last trap, I headed across the hills in the direction of the pasture where I would find the horses, one of which would be my mount for the ride home.

As it grew darker, the moon began to shine through the light clouds with an eerie, ghostlike glow. I remember the stillness—nothing to disturb the evening quietness. The only sound was the soft crunch of my boots in the snow. Not even a breath of wind broke the silence.

After walking for about thirty minutes, I realized I should have arrived at a point where a gate would let me into our own pasture. But something was wrong. I found no fence or gate. Continuing to search for them, a strange fear began to grip me. Why wasn't that gate where it was supposed to be? I thought I was walking in the right direction, and I also thought I had walked far enough, but that knowledge only made matters worse. Where was the gate that was supposed to be there? I was bewildered, for even though I felt certain that I had all the right answers, they just didn't seem to fit together.

Continuing in the dim moonlight, I suddenly came up against a fence. Now my concern increased. The fence seemed to be running east and west instead of north and south. Where was I? A strange sensation, a tingling fear slowly filled me from head to toe. I was lost!

Being lost cannot be described—it must be experienced.

It was the kind of feeling Dorothy and I had during those days in Hazelton when we began to realize that some of the things we had heard did not line up with the truths we were discovering in God's Word. Where are we? we asked.

After the initial shock of realizing I was lost on that cold winter night on the lonely prairie, my thoughts turned Godward. Having read stories of what panic and fear can do in such a situation, my whole being reached out, asking God for calm and a sense of direction. I felt impressed to follow the fence toward my left, and soon I found a gate. It appeared strange at first—not the one I was looking for. I began examining every detail that could be seen in the dim light until I recognized one of the corner posts. Some months before, while watching another farmer build his fence, I noticed a chip taken out of the corner post he used to hang the gate on. Recognizing that chip probably saved my life. The dim moon gave just enough light so I could see it. Following its direction I found my way home.

One small sign had been enough to lead me to safety. God had allowed me to find it so that I could get my bearings and find my way home. That notch on the gate post, small as it was, had great significance. This sign wasn't a place of safety—it merely pointed me to the place of safety.

In much the same way, many of the truths in the Old Testament are that kind of sign. They were given with the intention of leading us to the whole, more complete truth about God's provision for our salvation.

One such sign was the tabernacle and the worship which was instituted under Moses.

To prepare Israel for the transition from the reliance upon self to the new covenant ministration of the Holy Spirit, God gave them the sanctuary service, which is rich in symbolism about God's provision for us.

The physical layout of the ark of the covenant, for example, which was placed in the earthly sanctuary, could be said to symbolize the nature of Israel's spiritual status at that time, the position the Jews occupied then, as well as the eventual changes that would have to take place in their relationship to God.

When we understand how the separation between man and God developed, we can avoid making the same mistakes Israel made. Paul wrote: "Now all these things happened unto them for ensamples: and they are written for our admonition, upon whom the ends of the world are come" (1 Cor. 10:11). Paul was referring to the sins and failures of Israel which had caused God to place a veil between himself and his people because he could no longer look upon them face to face.

The key to the sanctuary service was the ark of the covenant, above which hovered the Shekinah glory, the divine presence which appeared as a brilliant cloud by day and a burning cloud at night, illuminating the inner sanctuary, the holy of holies. The ark represented the presence and holiness of God. No man could stand or enter into its presence except the priests appointed to care for the tabernacle and minister as mediators between God and man. The principle of total separation between a holy God and all things sinful was never illustrated more concisely than in the physical layout of the ark and its contents.

INSIDE THE ARK

The ark contained three articles: a golden pot of manna, Aaron's rod that budded, and the two stone tablets of the law (Heb. 9:4). All three of these articles held major significance in the way God was dealing with his people. But, because of the sinful nature of the people of Israel, they committed a major sin against God in each of these significant areas. As a result, these three articles bore testimony against them. Deep in the recesses of the ark, shut away from the penetrating rays of the Shekinah glory, lay the three emblems reminding Israel of their sinfulness.

The Pot of Manna. The golden pot containing the manna represented God's provision which his people rejected. The first major sin which Israel committed was their complaining about God's provision. Their sin brought the first separation between Israel and God. As we have seen earlier, it was the plan of God to deliver them from Egyptian bondage, and take them to a land flowing with milk and honey. He purposed to be their total provider. He longed to become their source of supply. He provided for them and desired to give them permanent rest, to remove the sentence under which they were compelled to eat bread by the sweat of their faces (Gen. 3:17-19). That God intended to supply all their physical needs as he originally did for Adam is evidenced by the fact that for forty years in the wilderness he supernaturally provided their food, their water, and kept their clothes and shoes from wearing out. As

Nehemiah wrote later: "Yea, forty years didst thou sustain them in the wilderness, so that they lacked nothing; their clothes waxed not old, and their feet swelled not" (Neh. 9:21).

The golden pot of manna inside the ark of the covenant was placed there as a witness to Israel's rejection of their God as their source of supply. They would not accept God as their total provision and turned to servitude under the curse of sin, where they could continue to eat bread by the sweat of their own faces. The pot of manna was preserved as a witness against them.

In John 6:31-35, Jesus gave the parallel of the manna and himself as the living bread which came down from heaven. The Jews were given another chance when Jesus revealed himself to them in the flesh, but again they rejected the true manna and turned to the provision they could make for themselves.

The Rod that Budded. The rod of Aaron was a symbol of God's authority and rulership to Israel. The record of Korah, Dathan, and Abiram (Num. 16, 17) tells of how these three men rose up against the authority of God which was vested in Moses and Aaron. They hoped to undermine God's government through these men and set themselves up as rulers of the people.

To verify his choice of leaders, God instructed Moses to cause every tribe to bring a rod and place them before the Lord. Eleven rods remained as dead as when they were brought, but the rod of Aaron was caused to bear buds, blossoms, and almonds simultaneously. By that miracle, God taught Israel that he alone reserved the right to appoint leaders of his people.

Israel was never satisfied with God's choices. By rejecting God's appointed leaders, they were rejecting God from being their head. The rod of Aaron, symbolizing God's authority, was given a permanent place in the ark of the covenant and remained a reminder of Israel's rejection of God's leadership (1 Sam. 8:6, 7).

The Tables of the Law. The third item placed inside the ark, away from the Shekinah glory, was the ten commandment laws written by God on two tables of stone. These laws itemized some of the major areas in which Israel had turned away from, and sinned against God. The pot of manna and Aaron's rod that budded illustrated two areas of rebellion not dealt with by the law on stone. The three items preserved inside the ark, together, covered all the areas of Israel's rebellious history.

The first three commandments pointed out to the people that they: (1) continued to revert back to the worship of other gods, (2) continued to create and worship graven images, and (3) they were taking the name of God upon their lips while their lives were proof that they carried that name in vain. In the midst of the decalogue stood the fourth commandment. This command summarized the tragic result of Israel's sin. It reminded them of the Rest in God which they forfeited by refusing to trust him.

The remainder of the ten commandments, five through ten, were a testimony which found every person guilty of not loving his neighbor as himself. All sinned and came short of the perfection God offered to them as the free work of grace. Their idle boast: "All that the Lord hath spoken we will do" only added to their guilt (Exod. 19:8).

The fifth commandment, to honor parents, stood as a witness against Israel, because none had fulfilled its challenge. The final three verses of the Old Testament are a testimony that this command to honor parents was never fulfilled. Malachi pointed to the coming of the Spirit of Elijah, the Holy Spirit, who would eventually do that which was impossible for man to do.

> Remember the law of Moses my servant . . . . Behold, I am going to send you Elijah the prophet before the coming of the great and terrible day of the Lord. And he will restore the hearts of the fathers to their children, and the hearts of the children to their fathers, lest I come and smite the land with a curse.
> [Mal. 4:4-6, NASB]

The sixth commandment found all men guilty, for as Jesus said, even anger without a cause is sufficient grounds to condemn a man.

The seventh commandment also convicted them, for none could claim that he never played the harlot by turning his affections to the allurements of the world. In the flesh, all men are guilty of spiritual adultery.

The stealing of time, opportunities or the credit that belongs to another is as wrong as stealing a neighbor's goods. This eighth command stood as a witness against Israel, condemning them to death.

The ninth commandment, forbidding falsehood of any kind, was another link in the chain which was designed to convince man of the hopelessness of salvation through human attainment.

The last of the decalogue, "Thou shalt not covet," is contrary to natural man's instinct. All Israel fell short of the demands of the law inscribed on the tablets of stone. The law stood as a witness against them, as did Aaron's rod and the pot of manna.

THE MERCY SEAT

The lid, or covering for the ark, was overlaid with gold, and stood as a representation of the mercy of God extended to his people. "Through the tender mercies of our God; whereby the dayspring from on high hath visited us" (Luke 1:78). In a place which represented God's holiness and witnessed to man's sinfulness, God desired to show mercy, as the coming of Jesus demonstrated.

THE LAWS OF SACRIFICES

In contrast to the pot of manna, Aaron's rod that budded, and the ten commandments, which were kept inside the ark, was the book of the law. God told Moses to place it beside the ark. Scholars are not certain how much of the writings of Moses were included in that book. It seems evident, however, that since the numerous laws God gave to Israel were not placed inside the ark, they were probably included in the book Moses placed outside the ark.

"Take this book of the law and place it beside the ark of the covenant of the Lord your God, that it may remain there as a witness against you" (Deut. 31:26, NASB).

The laws of sacrifices were the symbol ordained of God to convey to his people the hope of redemption, and freedom from the power of sin, through the Messiah. Those laws did two things: (1) They represented God's pledge of victory over Satan and sin to all who practiced them by faith and (2) they warned the unrepentant of eternal death under the curse of the law.

The laws of sacrifices which pointed the repentant to forgiveness in Christ also pointed the willful sinner to damnation and hell. The application of this two-pronged message is realized in the New Testament: "To the latter it seems like the deathly smell of doom, to the former it has the refreshing fragrance of life itself" (2 Cor. 2:16, Phillips). Elsewhere, in the Old Testament, the same truth is reflected: "A blessing, if you obey the commandments of the Lord your God, which I command ye this day: and a curse, if ye will not obey the commandments of the Lord your God, but turn aside out of the way which I command you" (Deut. 11:27, 28).

God offered forgiveness to Israel. Moses recorded God's plan for entering into his forgiveness and placed it at the side of the ark. But Israel would not obey. God knew the law on stone was beyond their capability to perform. He also knew they would reject the Lamb of God to whom the sacrificial laws pointed. These same laws meant death to all who rejected the salvation which was available. Eventually they stood as a witness against the whole nation of Israel because they rejected the Christ to whom the laws directed them. Because they rejected his blood, their own blood would be required.

When Christ purchased our redemption with his blood, he

also "canceled the written code, with its regulations, that was against us and that stood opposed to us; he took it away, nailing it to the cross" (Col. 2:14, NIV).

Because God had written in his own handwriting the legal decrees on the tables of stone, they could not be removed except by the blood of Jesus. They stood inside the ark as a testimony that Israel had sinned.

But when Jesus died, God not only forgave men their sins, but he also removed the reminders of sin which he caused Moses to preserve inside the ark as a witness against them.

THE CHERUBIM

On the top of the mercy seat were fashioned two cherubim or angels (Exod. 25:18). These represented the angels of God who were commissioned to act as communicants between God and man.

Throughout the history of Israel, angels were used to communicate the will of God to men. Balaam was stopped by an angel when on his way to curse Israel. Manoah and his wife were visited by an angel, who announced the coming birth of Samson. Gideon was directed by an angel of God to lead Israel to victory against the Midianites. Daniel was visited by angels who gave him prophecies, and interpretations of visions regarding the future history of the world. Zacharias was told by an angel that John the Baptist would be born. Mary, the mother of Jesus, was visited by an angel. The shepherds heard the angels' proclamation at the birth of Jesus.

In the days before Moses, God often visited his people without intermediaries. Enoch walked and talked with God. God talked with Abraham (Gen. 12—22). But when Israel turned away from God, a veil was put between them and the Lord; they shut themselves away from direct communion with him. The people said unto Moses, "Speak thou with us, and we will hear: but let not God speak with us, lest we die" (Exod. 20:19).

THE VEIL

From that time, when Moses put a veil over his face as a barrier between God's glory, which shone from his face after his appearance on the mountain, God was veiled from the people. Veil after veil was erected, separating the people farther and farther from their God. Some of the veils, or walls of separation, that were made necessary because of sin were:

The mercy seat, separating the ministration of death inside the ark from the ministration of glory above the ark.

The cherubim, which were symbolic of the angels who largely took over the task of visiting mankind.

Moses himself, who was asked to stand between God and his people. Moses thereafter had to veil his face because of the glory which was reflected from his meeting with God.

The levitical priesthood. Before Sinai, the head of each household was responsible to offer his own sacrifice for himself and for his family. One example was when the passover lamb was slain and the blood was sprinkled about the door of each house before the exodus from Egypt. God never intended for one man to serve as intermediary or priest for another man. Each man was responsible to be the priest for his own home.

Because Israel was unable to come to God for itself, God set up the levitical priesthood to stand between himself and the people.

The Temple Veil. When Jesus died, and the barrier was removed, the people of God could again enter into the presence of God in Jesus' name, boldly making their requests known directly to God. The writer of Hebrews encouraged believers: "Let us therefore come boldly unto the throne of grace, that we may obtain mercy, and find grace to help in time of need" (Heb. 4:16).

These words were written nearly two thousand years ago! Thus, I began to understand that the way into the holiest was not opened in 1844, as my former church was teaching, but when the veil in the temple was opened by God at the time of Christ's death. "Jesus, when he had cried again with a loud voice, yielded up the ghost. And behold, the veil of the temple was rent in twain from the top to the bottom; and the earth did quake, and the rocks rent; and the graves were opened; and many bodies of the saints which slept arose" (Matt. 27:50-52).

Some of the early leaders of my church, in calculating the dates of prophecy, concluded that Christ would return to earth in 1844. When that date came and went and Christ did not come, they concluded that something else must have occurred at that time and they believed it had to do with Christ entering into the holy of holies of heaven for our sakes.

Jesus' body. Another veil that shielded man from the glory of God was the human body of our Lord Jesus. When he died and was raised from the dead, he reopened the way that was blocked by sin and established direct access to God for us. To his disciples he said, "This is my body, which is broken for you: this do in remembrance of me." Simultaneously, the body of Jesus was broken and the veil in the temple was rent.

We should realize that the daily sacrifices of the earthly sanctuary symbolized the offerings presented by God's people, by faith in a coming Messiah, from the days of Moses until Christ died.

Even though those people received forgiveness, they understood that forgiveness was contingent on the eventual death of the Lamb of God. When the Lamb of God was slain, a perfect and final atonement was made. The antitypical day of atonement for the world was the day Jesus died for our sins. The day of atonement for the whole world caused an end to the continuous or daily sacrifices. Those sacrifices pointed to the great day when the need for further sacrifices would be ended.

A question might arise as to what point in time God the

Father accepted the sacrifice of Jesus as sufficient to redeem his people from all their sins. In other words, when was Jesus' role as our high priest and redeemer climaxed and ratified in heaven?

Some erroneously teach that this ratification took place after his resurrection. This is not possible, nor can it be true, because Satan would not have released any whom he had claimed through death unless Jesus' sacrifice had already been accepted by the Father. He first had to receive authority to release those whom Satan claimed as his own. The resurrection itself was proof of the fact that the sacrifice had been accepted.

Failure to understand the full significance of the resurrection has caused some to think that the daily services of the earthly sanctuary were typical of Christ's work on behalf of the sinners until 1844, and that only since that date are we in the antitypical day of the atonement. The New Testament teaches, however, that Jesus' blood once applied to the sinner, completely cleanses him. In the light of the teaching of Hebrews, one wonders why we would need to have the blood applied once to be forgiven, and then once more to be given the so-called "final atonement."

We realized how much we owed to those who through the years had faithfully taught us the Word of God. But we also learned the lesson of relying on the Holy Spirit to be our teacher and not to rely on the wisdom of man.

The Law on stone was given as a sign and a teacher to those who were in darkness. It was merely a pointer showing us the way to go home. But it was not *the way.* Jesus said he is *The Way.* A signpost, or a chip on a gatepost, cannot lead a person home, as that sign did for me that night. It can only point the way.

6
Resting in His Provision

Our family had been planning a holiday to Mexico for some time. Every aching bone in our bodies responded to the idea of a winter vacation in the sun. I was no longer teaching school at that time and we had gone into business for ourselves.

Following a very busy summer in our tourist and land development enterprise, we looked forward to finding a place where we could temporarily forget the pressures of life and have some fun and rest.

A portion of our lakeside acreage had been subdivided to help pay for the expense involved in developing a tourist recreation park business. Final government approval for a nineteen-lot subdivision was received just one month before the British Columbia government temporarily put a stop to all development along Highway 97. It had all worked out, step by step, so beautifully that we had no doubt that God's hand was in the situation. Permits which should have taken up to three months to receive had come through in half a day as God led me to take some short cuts which I was told would never work. Each move seemed to have been preplanned by God. It was so good, after years of hard slugging, to know God was again going to give us some visible guidance.

I had been juggling funds all summer, using business profits to finish work on the real estate project, and trusting that we would sell enough building lots before winter to take care of our living expenses and provide a much-needed vacation. It was just a matter of turning assets into cash. In rapid succession, three lots sold, providing funds to cover the yearly mortgage payment. We received a sizeable deposit on a fourth lot, and payment in full was to be made in three weeks. At last, we could relax and make arrangements for the holiday trip.

Delighted with having received a deposit on the fourth lot, we retired that night in a happy frame of mind, and I fell into a deep sleep.

I awoke suddenly in the middle of a dream, with all my senses responding to a very real awareness of the Lord's presence. Several times in the past nine years, I had had such experiences and had come to recognize that the Lord was about to bring something to pass in our lives. I had been dreaming that I was standing outside the travel agent's office, ready to hand him a check for the prearranged Mexican holiday. A puff of wind had blown the check out of my hand, and I had the strange feeling of it pulling out of my fingers even though I tried desperately to hold onto it. I dashed after the flying piece of paper, and each time my fingers reached it, the same gust of wind blew it farther down the street. Then I awoke and in my heart I knew immediately that the fourth lot sale would not go through, that I would have to return the deposit, and that we would be with no funds to live on, much less for a vacation.

Mercifully, the Lord was preparing me for the shock. He was also readying me for one of the greatest teaching experiences of my life, saying, "Trust me!"

Three days later, the prospective buyer phoned to say that

he was being transferred unexpectedly to a distant city and would have to cancel plans for building a home in this area. He knew that normally a deposit is forfeited, but he requested my consideration in these circumstances which were beyond his control. Knowing what the Lord expected me to do, I decided to return the deposit in full. We canceled the trip, and began what was to become a unique three-month vigil of waiting upon the Lord. From the Word, the Spirit had taught me *about* entering into rest. Now from experience, he was going to let our faith become reality. "Happy—blessed, fortunate [enviable]—is the man who finds skillful and godly Wisdom, and the man who gets understanding—drawing it forth [from God's Word and life's experiences] (Prov. 3:13, Amp.).

Up to this time, my wife Dorothy had been my co-worker in almost every undertaking of life—the ministry, building two houses, and designing and sculpting displays for our tourist park. God, who had provided for us, had been dealing with her very distinctly regarding her role in our marriage. The Lord was reminding her of the bride and the bridegroom—the Church and her Lord—and how he had promised to provide for her and supply all her needs "according to his riches in glory" (Phil. 4:19).

Together, Dorothy and I always looked to God to do this, and now God was about to deal with us very specifically in this area. The Lord began to teach Dorothy about the provision for her through her husband. I was depending on her help more than I should have, and on the other hand, she felt that without her direct contribution, we might not have sufficient funds to get along on. God was beginning to teach us that without his blessing, all our efforts would come to nothing anyway.

The husband is the earthly picture of the provider, God. God designed marriage to illustrate his relationship with us. Dorothy was beginning now to glimpse herself in a new role of ministering love and encouragement to her husband, and trusting the Giver of all good gifts to provide for all our financial needs through her husband.

We were created for God's pleasure. He desires that we minister unto him our love, our adoration, worship, and praise, and trust him to do the work of transforming us. Then he uses the transformed persons as a witness to the world about himself and his transforming power. As an artist displays his abilities by putting his work on exhibition, so "we are his workmanship, created in Christ Jesus unto good works, which God hath before ordained that we should walk in them" (Eph. 2:10). In another place Paul wrote that "we should be to the praise of his glory" (Eph. 1:12).

The Christian—the bride—is to believe in her Lord and trust him as her provider. As she has confidence in her husband's ability, and in God to provide through him, her own role is elevated to that of loving and resting in the provision guaranteed by God. Dorothy and I had learned all this in theory, and had occasions to trust him for other things. Now we were given another real-life opportunity to learn specific lessons about resting and trusting.

With or without the dream, whether sent by God or coincidental as some skeptics may have thought it was, we knew that we were under God's control and that nothing happened without his permission. Because of their subjective nature, such experiences are difficult to deal with objectively in discussing them with others. God has many ways to teach his people. We believed that my dream was the way he chose to teach us.

We refused to accept that we were to be made prisoners of the circumstances or by the enemy because the property hadn't sold. Paul never recognized himself as a prisoner of Rome when he was jailed for his testimony—he knew he was where he was by God's appointment. He believed that God was working all things for good (Rom. 8:28). We also believed that God had something good for us in this. The wind that blew the check out of my hand was under the control of the one who controls all the winds and waves.

Since my work load was already committed to a business which would not again be financially productive until the following spring, I could not abandon our investment and look for other employment. The subdivision was covered by snow, and nothing short of a miracle would bring a land buyer, to buy a piece of property which he could not see before spring.

Dorothy's usual reaction to such circumstances would be immediately to start looking for a job herself. Inexplicably, she felt the restraining hand of God and shared with me that she felt this was a personal test for her to trust God to provide through her husband. To have several hundred thousand dollars in assets frozen by bad weather and circumstances was ridiculous enough for laughter and serious enough for tears.

At church, during the next prayer service, Dorothy and I both felt the presence of God in an unusual way. On the way to church I had said out loud: "God, what do we do now?"

As we prayed and worshiped the Lord, a deep sense of peace settled over us, a soothing balm filled us. That night a message was given, showing that God was leading us upon the mountaintop as well as in the valley. We were not to worry or wonder what to do, for the Lord would show us in his time.

The pastor then opened the Word to Ephesians 3:1, and Ephesians 4:1, where Paul described himself as the prisoner of Jesus Christ. Not once did Paul consider himself anyone's prisoner except the Lord's. We accepted this as further confirmation that we were in God's hands and that we should trust in him. We really were in a deep valley—a prison—but God was shedding so much light on our pathway that we felt we were on a mountain top with him. It was cause for praise.

In learning to praise God, we found that we were lifted above the circumstances from where Satan's darts were hurled at us. The sound of praise daily lifted us up above the prison of doubt, fear, and perplexity, to a higher level where God made his presence known. It was wonderful to find ourselves feeling free and happy, even though we had no money in the bank. We knew that our Father had more than enough and that he loved us.

The windowed envelopes continued to arrive in the mail, making us increasingly aware of regular monthly financial obligations which weren't being met. One of these was the oil bill. Our oil tank had been filled regularly by the same supplier since we built the house. He appreciated our prompt payments even as we appreciated his service. He had filled our five-hundred-gallon tank on December tenth. At the end of January the measuring stick showed that the tank was just slightly more than one-third full. Running true to schedule, I knew that by March tenth, it would be nearly empty and due for a refill. I didn't have the money to pay for the December tenth filling, and company policy required that we pay for the earlier filling before we received another delivery. So we just trusted that somehow we would keep warm.

At the end of February I measured again. The tank was still one-third full! In a month of cold weather, it looked as if we had used hardly any oil at all. Either I hadn't measured correctly, or we were, by being careful, using much less oil, or God was supplying in some other way. Finally in May, when the tank was filled, it took exactly three hundred fifty-nine gallons, which means that it was still nearly one-third full! We are keeping the delivery slip as a souvenir of God's love to us.

Our eldest son remarked that it sounded like the Bible story about Elijah and the widow's cruse of oil that kept pouring out oil until all the vessels were filled.

The way our oil supply held up through the winter was typical of how the Lord provided for us that year. In order for us to break out of our financial prison, we needed to sell just one piece of property—one building lot. The Lord had allowed us to lose the down payment on that lot and had graciously explained that he was allowing it and that he was still in control. God never takes from us without returning much more than he has taken. We stood on the threshold of a thrilling spiritual discovery.

One day friends invited us to their home to share a day of prayer and to listen to some tapes they had received from someone in California. The speaker, in giving an explanation of Matthew 16:19, opened our eyes to a possibility we hadn't considered before. Matthew recorded Jesus saying, "And I will give unto thee the keys of the kingdom of heaven: and whatsoever thou shalt bind on earth shall be bound in heaven: and whatsoever thou shalt loose on earth shall be loosed in heaven."

The speaker on the tape, almost as if he knew we would be listening to him said, "Do you have a piece of property that you cannot sell?" We sat bolt upright as we heard those words.

The speaker went on to say that the reason such a situation might exist was that Satan might be hindering the potential buyer to keep the sale from going through. If that were the case, God's work or God's people could be hindered as a result. We had never considered it in such a way.

Believing that the sale of the property was the way we were going to make it financially, we began praying for a buyer in a new way. If Satan was hindering the person who needed the property (certainly God wouldn't make someone buy it who didn't need it just so we could have the money), we asked that this attack of Satan be defeated. We began to pray that the buyer, whoever he was, would be released from the control of the enemy, if that was the reason a buyer wasn't forthcoming. Our friends joined with us as we prayed to that end.

Soon after that prayer meeting, our eldest son's wife, Lynn, dreamed that we sold a lot, and that the date of the sale was three days before the end of March.

Our family business now included our married son David and Lynn, his wife, our daughter Linda and her husband Elmer, and our youngest son Robert, who helped after school. Because of the financial stress we were all under, we were drawn together as we never were before. As we worked in the shop, we would sing and pray and listen to teaching tapes.

Love continued to flow more deeply among our extended family. We even shared our meals together. Often the three families would combine resources and cook in the same pot.

It was a great way to learn to share and to stand together. In this way, we found there was plenty to eat. An amply-supplied deep freeze was a real blessing because our cash had long since run out and our buying was reduced to a minimum. As our supplies dwindled, we were aware of a distinct change in the quality of our love and the peace and joy we were experiencing. We found ourselves laughing and admitting to one another that, if we had to choose between release from our financial problems or giving up the spiritual blessings God was giving us, we would far rather forsake all things than to lose the joy we were experiencing together.

An example of the caring that developed among us was when Lynn, who was expecting their first baby, offered to give us the money she had saved as a nest egg for the birth of the child. Although we didn't accept her offer, we realized that God was literally turning the hearts of the children to the fathers (Mal. 4:6).

Another test came one day when we received an unsolicited letter from a finance company saying that we had an A-1 credit rating and could borrow sufficient funds to carry us through until the new tourist season. After discussing the offer with the entire family, we agreed to reject it because to accept it would mean bailing ourselves out of a situation in which we knew God had purposefully placed us. To accept it would amount to short-circuiting God's plan before he had completed the work he was doing in us. We didn't wish to take a repeat course in the same lesson later. We determined to wait upon God. Just as he was able to place us in the difficult situation, he was able to set us free from it. We wanted the same Holy Spirit who blew the check out of my hand to blow another one in, so we continued to wait and praise God for what he was doing.

Toward the end of March, I had another dream in which I saw a beautiful fish swimming slowly against the current up a stream. It was headed up the stream to where there was a little hollowed-out nest in the gravel. As the water became shallower, the fish hesitated, then after eyeing the nesting spot, he darted for it and settled in with a very happy, satisfied look on his face. (I don't know how a fish can look happy, but in my mind's eye, this one did.)

I awakened very suddenly and wondered if it wasn't another indication that the Lord was about to do something for us, giving another premonition like the one I thought I had received when the deal fell through the previous fall. Dorothy woke up and wanted to know what I was so excited about. I told her about the dream and suggested that it might mean that one of the lots might sell very soon.

"How do you know?" she inquired sleepily. "You woke me up to tell me about a fish with a nesting urge, and want me to believe it means someone is wanting to buy one of the lots?" I could tell she thought that I was overanxious and overreacting to everything.

She turned over and went back to sleep. I thought it over and realized how silly I must have sounded. Yet, even though my mind rejected the idea, in my heart I felt it was real. Then I turned over and went back to sleep.

But "the foolishness of God is wiser than men . . . . God hath chosen the foolish things of the world to confound the wise; and God hath chosen the weak things of the world to confound the things which are mighty" (1 Cor. 1:25, 27).

I won't ever forget March 29. The snow was fast receding under the bright rays of spring sunshine. Our whole family was in the park, sculpting another life-sized animal for our display section when a car drove up to the subdivision. I had watched so many cars drive up there and had talked to so many people with no results that I just said: "If he is God's man, God can do the selling. I'll just mind my business and not get in the way." About two hours later the same car drove down again and, seeing us, the driver came over and asked to speak to the owner.

"What can I do for you?" I asked.

"How much is lot number eighteen?" he inquired.

We went up to the house, and about half an hour later, he left with an interim contract. And in my hand was a check for a good down payment on the lot, with promise of the balance to be paid upon transfer of the title.

By this time, the family work crew had ceased sculpting and was, by turn, praying that God would undertake while I was talking to the potential buyer. When I went back and announced that God had opened the prison gates and had set us free, we cried, danced, and shouted as our joy overflowed.

Then somebody remembered Lynn's dream. It had happened on the very date that she told us it would—three days before the end of the month. Believing this was from the Lord, we had more cause to praise the Lord.

Then Dorothy came to me with tears in her eyes and said she was sorry for doubting, but admitted that she still did not see how a fish related to the sale of the lot.

The following morning I prepared to go to the bank to cash the check, but first I went to the kitchen and told Dorothy to take her first good look at the check with which God had set us free. She took one look at it and came so near to fainting that she almost collapsed on the floor.

"What's the matter, dear?" I asked.

"Did you see it?" she shouted. "Did you see it?"

"See what? What are you talking about?" I inquired.

"No, you didn't see it, did you? God had held your eyes from seeing the name on the check in order that I might learn to believe," she sobbed.

"Look at that signature!" she cried.

"Fish! Fish!" we both called out together.

The signature was "Art Fish."* Throughout the excitement of the transaction, my mind failed to register the name of the man who bought the lot. Dorothy says she thinks God held my eyes until she might see and believe.

The dream—"the foolish things of this world to confound the wise." It made me wonder if God must not have fun as he deals with us.

I realized that the dreams the Lord gave us may not be the way he would guide everybody. Perhaps others don't need these signs to follow him, but I suppose God thought that we needed some kind of compensation or consolation, so he gave them to us.

But we learned again the lesson he had been teaching us for some time. We saw again that the Lord was serious when he said, "Come to Me, all you who labor and are heavy laden and over burdened, and I will cause you to rest" (Matt. 11:28, Amp.).

*Name used by permission.

7
The Two Ways

Years ago, travelers from Alberta to British Columbia used to turn north at the town of Golden, near the headwaters of the Columbia River, and follow the river on its treacherous and circuitous route of nearly two hundred miles to the town of Revelstoke. From there the road continued on into the interior of British Columbia. That road was called the Big Bend Highway because it followed the semicircle or bend made by the Columbia River as it flowed north and then turned south again to continue on into the United States.

Engineers who studied the mountainous terrain later built a new road from Golden, which went west through the Roger's Pass into Revelstoke. The new road was several hours shorter to travel than the old way.

When the new road was opened, a sign was placed at the entrance to the old route saying, "New Highway Now Open," with arrows indicating the new direction travelers were to take. Most of the travelers trusted the signs and took the new route and were able to cut several hours of travel time.

Yet, despite the new road being open, a few people insisted on using the old route. They had always done so. Having become accustomed to its treacherous hills and turns, they chose the familiar landmarks. After blowing a few more tires on the fallen rocks, some cautiously tried the new way and were overwhelmed by the contrast.

The same thing happened to those who loved the old Mosaic law. They felt like traitors to an old friend, so they refused to give up the old way rather than take the new way which faith in Jesus opened for them.

Just as the maintenance crews were pulled off the old Big Bend Highway and put to work on the new road, so Jesus caused his Spirit to be withdrawn from ministering under the Old Covenant and was sent to illumine the new and living way, the way for those who return from the old way to travel the highway of faith.

The travelers who go around the "Road Closed" sign and get onto the old road will find life increasingly barren and frustrating. God allows people to go the way they choose until they discover that the road becomes impossible. It took that for Israel to understand their need of a better way.

LEARNING TO TRUST

When God called Israel to go directly into Canaan by faith, they found it difficult to follow where they could not comprehend with their own minds. Rather than reject them because of their insistence on human understanding of what God was doing before they would obey, God put them on a detour around Mount Sinai. In the roundabout journey, they would learn that God's ways cannot be analyzed according to human logic.

To understand all of God's ways would require perfect knowledge—one would have to be as wise as God. Since that is impossible for any human, the Israelites had to learn to obey by faith and not act according to their own understanding. They were allowed to wander for forty years until they ceased trying to comprehend his ways and were willing to trust and obey him.

In a crisis there is often no time for discussion. Obedience must be immediate. Because the Christian walk is not according to human wisdom, God's way can best be understood in retrospect. Action must be taken by faith, based on what God is saying. Knowledge and wisdom come as a result of that kind of action. "Trust in the Lord with all thine heart; and lean not unto thine own understanding. In all thy ways acknowledge him, and he shall direct thy paths" (Prov. 3:5, 6).

God led Israel out of Egypt and showed them that he would provide for them. They were angry, afraid, and unbelieving, saying that God had made a mistake by leading them out into the desert to die.

God's response was to take them farther into the desert where the incorrigible unbelievers among them died off, those who would rather trust in their own logic than in God's wisdom. When the lessons were learned, God's first order was for Israel to cross the Jordan River, which was at flood stage during that season. Forty years earlier, under similar circumstances at the Red Sea they had balked and were ready to kill Moses. This time they marched forward toward the water as instructed. Just when it seemed that Joshua and the priests bearing the ark were about to lead them into a death march into the waters of the Jordan, the waters parted and they crossed on dry ground. In doing this, they passed faith test number one.

Next God ordered them to wage a very strange warfare against the first walled city of the land of Canaan. Rather than using human weapons, God asked them to do what would appear a very foolish thing—walk around the city every day for six days. They may have felt ridiculous doing their daily jog around the city like a bunch of school children playing follow the leader. Then on the seventh day of the march, God told Joshua to strike up the band and thank him for giving them the city. In some ways, this was more an act of faith than when Israel had faced a waterless desert forty years before. But they had learned that God does not always appeal to the brain or logic. He often uses what would appear foolish to the world to bring glory to his name. This time they were willing to risk making "fools" of themselves rather than disobey him again. The trumpeters were all in their places, waiting for the signal. The people of Jericho were probably watching from the city walls, fully armed for battle, and very puzzled by the strange behavior of the Israelites walking around their city. Contrary to all human reason, the walls of Jericho came down as the people shouted praise to God.

Israel had been on a detour, but now God was showing them the better way and bringing them back to the main highway of faith. They did not enter Canaan at first because they were trusting in their own abilities, but now they were entering because they were trusting in God. It was because of their obedience in believing God and acting on it that the waters of the Jordan River were stopped up and that the walls of Jericho came tumbling down.

For those who accept the way of faith, and rest in the works of Jesus, the way to the promised land is short and detours are unnecessary. We need not go by way of Mount Sinai, which is typified by Hagar and Ishmael, as the relationship to the law was described in Galatians:

> This contains an allegory: for these women are two covenants, one proceeding from Mount Sinai bearing children who are slaves; she is Hagar. Now this Hagar is Mount Sinai in Arabia, and corresponds to the present Jerusalem, for she is in slavery with her children. But the Jerusalem above is free; she is our mother. [Gal. 4:24-26, NASB]

Much of Paul's writings were to prevent people from taking the legalistic detour around Mount Sinai where they would die like Israel of old. Paul challenged them to trust God rather than themselves. Only those who get off the detour which goes around Mount Sinai, and find their way back to the way of faith, will be victorious against the giants who rise against them.

Even as we are delivered from our sins by faith, as Israel

was delivered from Egypt, so we must march on and live victorious lives by faith. The new way to the promised land may not be as broad or as well traveled as the detour, but it is a straight road.

According to Galatians 4:24, 25, God has two ways of helping people. We have seen that the covenant given to Moses at Mount Sinai, together with all its retinue of laws, did not represent God's primary plan of salvation.

The Mosaic covenant was designed so man had to approach God through an earthly mediator or priest. Man had no direct communion with God because the broken law stood between him and God. "All have sinned and come short of the glory of God" (Rom. 3:23). The law pointed out just how sinful man was.

Jesus was the only man who ever kept the law perfectly. God knew the impossibility of mankind ever satisfying the law on stone, so Jesus kept it for us, and became our righteousness. By doing so, he took the covenant written on stone and fulfilled it by his perfect life and perfect sacrifice as the Lamb of God. Then Jesus gave us his righteousness as a free gift "so by the obedience of one shall many be made righteous" (Rom. 5:19).

Having set us free from the law's demands, Jesus offers to his people a much higher standard of holiness than the law could ever prescribe. But with the higher standard of holiness, God provides through the indwelling Holy Spirit, a new means by which all may become holy and acceptable unto God.

> But if I depart, I will send him [the Holy Spirit] unto you. And when he is come, he will reprove the world of sin, and of righteousness, and of judgment: Of sin because they believe not on me; of righteousness, because I go to my Father, and ye see me no more; of judgment, because the prince of this world is judged. [John 16:7-11]

In this passage, the work of the Holy Spirit is described in several ways. First, the Spirit is responsible to teach men, to convict them of that which is sin in God's sight. The standard of righteousness is no longer the negative law on stone, but the positive law of faith and love which causes one to trust and obey God at all times.

The Holy Spirit came also to teach the meaning of true holiness which is far more than abstaining from evil. The Holy Spirit teaches us that there is no righteousness apart from Christ, since "all our righteousnesses are as filthy rags" (Isa. 64:6). The only righteousness God recognizes is that which his Son has purchased. The Spirit teaches us that in order to escape the judgment along with the prince of this world, the devil, we must be clothed with the wedding garment which is the gift of Christ's own righteousness. We dare not try to weave with human effort a covering for our sins. If we try to provide our own, like the guest at the wedding banquet, we will be cast out into the outer darkness (Matt. 22:11). Adam and Eve tried to make their own garments of fig leaves, which were inadequate. God clothed them with skins which required the shedding of blood, symbolic of the precious blood of Jesus which would one day be offered to cover their sins.

The Holy Spirit causes us to see Christ as he is so that we might see ourselves as we are. Only then can we turn to God that we might allow him to properly clothe us.

It comes as a surprise to some Christians to learn that few of the events recorded in the four Gospels were enacted during the New Covenant or New Testament era. The Old Testament dispensation did not end with Malachi, or even with Matthew chapter one, but with the end of Matthew when Christ died, and was raised from the dead. Likewise the New Testament or New Covenant era did not begin with the birth of Christ in Bethlehem's manger, but on Golgotha's hill when the Lamb of God died for the sins of the world and rose after three days as King of Kings.

The Jews in Paul's day were confused because, not recognizing Christ as the Messiah, they did not know that the laws and systems given to Moses at Sinai had fulfilled their purposes and come to an end. Paul emphasized the effective time element of the Sinai laws when he said, "Wherefore then serveth the law? It was added because of transgressions, till the seed should come" (Gal. 3:19).

Only when we understand that Christ himself was born and lived under the limitations of the Old Covenant, can we see that not everything he did in his lifetime was intended to be duplicated exactly by the Church after Pentecost. He was born under the Mosaic laws, lived under the Mosaic laws, and died under the Mosaic laws. Having successfully fulfilled the law, and having conquered sin on our behalf, the grave could not hold him. He went down into death on the Old Covenant side of time, and three days later rose from that grave on the New Covenant side of time.

Once we realize that the division between the Old and the New is marked not by birth, but by the death and resurrection of Christ, much of the confusion caused by mixing up the terms and conditions of the two covenants is cleared up. Christ did not introduce the New Covenant in his blood until just before his death when he instituted the Lord's Supper (Matt. 26:28, Amp.).

Jesus lived during the period of transition between the past and the future. In fact he was the Transition. He alone had the authority to bring down the curtain on the ritualism and legalism which was typical of the Old Testament religion, and to open the door to the new age of the ministration of the Holy Spirit. Jesus came to lead his people out of the legalistic darkness of the Old Covenant into the light of the New Covenant of grace.

It was part of Jesus' work to prepare his people to move beyond servitude to a code of written laws, and to look directly to God for guidance. Not that the Holy Spirit would lead contrary to the written code, but rather that he would open our eyes to see beyond the letter, and comprehend the *intent and spirit of that law.* "The letter kills," Paul said, "but the Spirit gives life."

THE LAW AND RIGHTEOUSNESS

Some may question the statement that the new life of faith

and love holds to higher standards than the ten commandments. The story which Christ told, which we call the parable of the Good Samaritan, might illustrate. Most will recall the story of the man who was traveling the perilous road from Jerusalem to Jericho, and was ambushed by robbers. He was assaulted, robbed, and left for dead by the wayside.

According to the story, a certain priest came by—a man of the temple—learned in the law. The priests placed great emphasis on living by the law, and upon seeing the unfortunate traveler, the priest no doubt considered his legal responsibility to the man.

We can picture the priest looking into the law to determine not only what he ought to do, but what he needn't do.

He considered the first four commandments. "No," he concluded, "these pertain to my worship of God, and do not have any bearing on this situation."

The next commandment says: "Honor thy father and thy mother." The priest may have reasoned that there was nothing in that which required him to help the beaten man. He went on.

"'Thou shalt not kill.' I certainly haven't killed anyone, and I won't do this man any further wrong."

"The seventh commandment has no bearing on this matter."

"'Thou shalt not steal.' Certainly I wouldn't do that," he continued. "I'm sorry he was robbed, but I didn't do it."

"The ninth commandment says, 'Thou shalt not bear false witness against thy neighbor,' so just to play it safe, I won't even speak to him."

"Covet? No, I don't envy him, nor do I covet anything he has! I'm in the clear!" And so saying, he went his way. Could these have really been his thoughts? Of course, we don't know. But we do read that he passed on the other side and did nothing to help.

Along came a Levite, a man of the tribe commissioned in

that age to stand as guardians of truth and righteousness. Surely, we think, here is a man who does the will of God. But he too, "looked on him" and passed by. Why? Could his thoughts have been akin to those of his brother the priest?

"The letter killeth, but the spirit giveth life" (2 Cor. 3:6). In a court of law, a good attorney would have won an easy acquittal for both the priest and the Levite if they had been accused of breaking the law. But the law of love was far from either of them.

Those who live by the law of love will not only desist from doing wrong or harm, as did the priest and the Levite, but will go far beyond the call of duty and show love to those in need. "By this shall all men know that ye are my disciples, if ye have love one to another" (John 13:35).

THE LAW TODAY

As we have seen from the story of the Good Samaritan, abstaining from evil does not make us a child of God. The ten commandments were largely a series of don'ts. It is significant that God wrote them on cold, impersonal, and unfeeling stones. Jesus indicated that to observe only legalistic codes was tantamount to washing a cup on the outside, or to whitewashing the outside of a sepulcre hoping thereby to eliminate the dirt and decay from inside.

While the old covenant law dealt with the symptoms of sin, the new covenant deals with the cause of sin. The ten commandments were given to convince all men that they needed a savior. Once we are convinced of our sinfulness and our need of a savior, the purpose of the law is fulfilled, according to the teachings of Galatians.

The law, as a schoolmaster, could educate the intellect and lead to an outward compliance with its requirements, but the law could not change a sinner into a child of God.

To tell a convert to Christianity today that God requires him to keep the ten commandments is to mislead him, because the law does not focus his attention on the source of victory, which is the Holy Spirit that indwells his heart. Such counsel would teach Christians to major in minors.

When the rich young ruler told Jesus that he had kept all the ten commandments from his youth up (he probably hadn't), he yet admitted that something was still missing. Jesus had made his point. Jesus showed him that even if he could keep the law, he would still be lacking.

Paul spoke of those who were under the coercion of the law as children, not yet old enough to appreciate the freedom that comes with spiritual maturity. When Jesus came, in the fulness of time, he redeemed us from the authority of the law and made us heirs as mature sons. We are no longer under the old tutor, the law of Moses, but under the authority of God's Spirit. Let no one who may be inclined to carnality suppose that the new Master, the Holy Spirit, is less demanding of holiness than the old laws were. On the contrary, the Holy Spirit demands a perfection which the law could never even describe, let alone attain to.

The primary difference in operation between the law and the Holy Spirit is that the laws began on the outside and worked inward. The Holy Spirit begins inside and works outward. The laws given on stone were seen or heard with the senses, entered into the mind, and there created an awareness of man's sin and his need. The Holy Spirit enters directly into the heart or spirit of man. He deals with the inner man first. The law washes the outside of the cup (Matt. 23:25). The Holy Spirit cleanses the inside, then the outward actions of love and compassion become a true expression of the inward work of grace. Man cannot by his efforts, however noble, duplicate the fruit of the Spirit which is "love, joy, peace, longsuffering, gentleness, goodness, faith, meekness, temperance" (Gal. 5:22).

THE LAW AND THE SABBATH

Paul wrote to the Galatians: "Ye observe days, and months, and times, and years. I am afraid of you, lest I have bestowed upon you labour in vain" (Gal. 4:10, 11). In another place, Paul wrote: "One man esteemeth one day above another: another esteemeth every day alike. Let every man be fully persuaded in his own mind. He that regardeth the day, regardeth it unto the Lord; and he that regardeth not the day, to the Lord he doth not regard it. He that eateth, eateth to the Lord, for he giveth God thanks; and he that eateth not, to the Lord he eateth not, and giveth God thanks" (Rom. 14:5, 6).

There is no point in trying to fog over the true teaching of Paul here by beginning an argument of whether or not the weekly Sabbath was included in this admonition. All we need to do is read what Paul himself said in the same chapter of Galatians.

In verses 21 through 24, Paul compares all the laws given at Sinai, the ten commandments plus the ceremonial laws, to Hagar, the bondwoman who bore a son for Abraham in the ordinary course of nature. The covenant given to Abraham, Paul compares to Sarah, whose son was born after the will of God.

Abraham first tried to help God fulfill the promise by assisting, or as he thought, cooperating with God. But all such efforts were rejected because they were tainted by works of man, and were not the works of God.

Then after Sarah was past the years of childbearing, God told Abraham the time had arrived. But Abraham laughed.

Taking Hagar was an example of the intellect getting in the way of faith. So was his laughing. Abraham's reason told him that God had waited too long. Even faithful Abraham had his moments of intellectual doubt, so we shouldn't feel too bad when we have such lapses. But even though he laughed within himself he believed God and did not faint at the promise.

According to the ordinary course of nature, we might say that Abraham and Sarah had nothing to do with the conception of Isaac. It was God who performed the double miracle and caused the son of promise to be born, not by the will of man, but by the will of God. According to the record in Galatians, Abraham had reasoned that since God had promised him a son, it would be ridiculous to just sit by and wait for a miracle. Once he knew that God planned to give him a son, he decided to prove his faith by his works. He would do all he could, and God would make up the difference. So since Sarah was barren, and God had given them a faithful servant, Hagar, they reasoned that if Sarah could only be unselfish and not too possessive of Abraham, they could help fulfill God's promise. Sarah made the suggestion and Abraham accepted. Hagar conceived by Abraham.

Paul in Galatians made something of a parallel with Abraham and Hagar's child to the law given at Sinai. When God called the Israelites to be his people and to obey him that he might fulfill his purpose for the world through them, their confidence was based on their ability rather than on the power of God. "All that the Lord hath spoken we will do" (Exod. 19:8). It seemed the emphasis was on the "we will do."

Just as with Hagar and the fruit of that carnal union—Ishmael—God could not accept the fruit of the works of the law because it was tainted by human effort. That is why we are told that by the works of the law shall no flesh be justified. Only that which is totally the works of God is acceptable to God.

Just as the fruit of the union of Abraham and Hagar was rejected by God before Ishmael was born, so also the law and its works were unacceptable. Paul directly compares the casting out of Hagar to the rejection of the law which leads to bondage. Neither Abraham's union with Hagar nor the giving of the law at Sinai were part of God's original plan for his people's salvation, and were destined for rejection before they were even given.

Speaking of the old covenant, Paul wrote:

> This is my argument: The Law, which began four hundred and thirty years after the covenant

> [concerning the coming Messiah], does not *and* can not annul the covenant previously established (ratified) by God, so as to abolish the promise *and* make it void. For if the inheritance [of the promise depends on observing] the Law [as these false teachers would like you to believe], it no longer [depends] on the promise; however God gave it to Abraham [as a free gift solely] by virtue of His promise. What then was the purpose of the Law? It was added—later on, after the promise, to disclose and expose to men their guilt—because of transgressions *and* [to make men more conscious of the sinfulness] of sin; and it was intended to be in effect until the Seed (the Descendant, the Heir) should come, to *and* concerning Whom the promise had been made. And it (the Law) was arranged *and* ordained and appointed through the instrumentality of angels [and was given] by the hand (in the person) of a go-between—an intermediary person (Moses) between God and man. [Gal. 3:17-19, Amp.]

This text shows that the reason why God gave the law was to convict Israel of their guilt and to make them conscious of their sinfulness. Having convicted them as sinners, the law as the schoolmaster pointed them to Christ (Gal. 3:24). God gave the law to remain in effect until Christ, the Seed, should come as the Redeemer. Having fulfilled its function, the law has been taken out of the way. As Paul wrote to the Colossians, "You . . . hath he quickened . . . having forgiven you all trespasses; blotting out the handwriting of ordinances that was against us, which was contrary to us, and took it out of the way, nailing it to his cross" (Col. 2:13, 14).

During the years when I pastored, I read texts like 2 Corinthians 3:7, and I truly thought that the "ministration of death written and engraven in stone" was something other than the ten commandments. I did not see how the law could be called the ministration of death if it was elsewhere described as holy, and just, and good.

We were taught that it was only the sacrificial laws that were taken out of the way and nailed to the cross. I was thoroughly shocked when I realized that I had failed to see a simple truth in Galatians 3:17: "the law, which was four hundred and thirty years after, cannot disannul, that it should make the promise of none effect." I asked myself which laws began four hundred and thirty years after the covenant made with Abraham. Not the law of sacrifices, for the sacrifices were first taught to Adam and were practiced by God's people till Noah, and on to the days of Abraham. Instructions about sacrifice were obviously given long before the covenant made with Abraham. Clearly, then, the sacrificial principle which pointed to the cross was not first given to Moses and could not have been the law referred to in Galatians 3:17.

Another point I never allowed my mind to dwell on was the question of how the sacrificial offerings could be thought of as having been "against us," for they were the one practice that pointed men to Christ and gave them hope. The sacrifices did not condemn the repentant sinner, since they were symbolic of the coming Messiah and gave men a reason for living. Each time a lamb was sacrificed, the sinner indicated his gratefulness to God for the way of escape. The lamb's death pointed to the coming Lamb of God whose death certainly never condemned the repentant sinner.

What then was the "ministration of death?" I asked. It must have been the "handwriting of ordinances" which Jesus nailed to the cross that was ministering death. The handwriting was God's handwriting on the tables of stone. The law condemned men to death, "because all who have sinned under the law will be judged and condemned by the law" (Rom. 2:12). And "all have sinned, and come short of the glory of God" (Rom. 3:23). And "the wages of sin is death" (Rom 6:23). As Ezekiel said, "The soul that sinneth, it shall die" (Ezek. 18:20). God knew that there was no way to save man from his sinful condition except through the death of his Son to whom the sacrifices pointed.

It is clear that no one is justified in God's sight by obeying the law, for "the righteous shall live by faith." To those who think that one is justified by faith, but then must prove his faith by keeping the law, Paul says, "Surely you can't be so stupid as to think that you begin your spiritual life in the Spirit and then complete it by reverting to physical observances?" (Gal. 3:3, Phillips).

God's real plan of salvation was given to Israel the same as it was to Adam, to Abraham, and to us. Salvation by faith meant to every generation that the believer should trust and act on the basis of what God said.

The law was never intended as an alternate way of salvation. It only promised Israel death, and was called the ministration of death. It was designed to do the good, and holy, and perfect work of converting the soul, and leading the converted one—the one who was arrested and turned around—to the One who alone could save them.

We have often seen a highway, blocked by a rock slide, closed for repairs. To accommodate the traffic, a temporary road is set up around the area of reconstruction. When the main road is repaired and again open to traffic, the detour is not necessarily destroyed. It is merely closed off and remains as a reminder that it was once used. Likewise, God's original plan for man was temporarily set aside until man could be convinced that he could not save himself. Then when by the death and resurrection of Christ the main road was cleared of the debris of sin, the Sinai detour had served its purpose and was closed off. Man was again free to fellowship with his God on the New and Living Way. Paul wrote:

> Now this true story is an illustration of God's two ways of helping people. One way was by giving them his laws to obey. He did this on Mount Sinai, when he gave the Ten Commandments to Moses. Mount Sinai, by the way, is called "Mount Hagar" by the Arabs—and in my illustration Abraham's slave-wife Hagar represents Jerusalem, the mother-city of the

Jews, the center of that system of trying to please God by trying to obey the Commandments; and the Jews, who try to follow that system, are her slave children. But our mother-city is the heavenly Jerusalem, and she is not a slave to Jewish laws. [Gal. 4:24-26, TLB]

8 Resting During the Storm

The first ocean trip my wife and I ever took was our crossing the Queen Charlotte Sound, north of Vancouver Island. Soon after we left the port, we began to run into rough waters. We were sailing in a converted World War II corvette, and as the sailors later explained, those boats had a built-in capacity to pitch and toss in heavy seas.

The storm struck at night with full force from the open Pacific and we felt we were alternately standing on our heads and then on our feet. The beds rolled from side to side, then up and down. The waves pounded the walls of the ship like sledgehammers. Needless to say, our stomachs kept us awake most of the night. With the coming of dawn, we ventured onto the deck to see what was happening.

I'll never forget the sight of the mountainous swells, which rolled higher than the ship, then seemed to slip underneath the boat, lifting us high into the air, then letting us slide down again on the other side of the waves. We noticed that each large wave or swell was made up of many smaller waves, all flowing together. With tremendous force and violence, they moved relentlessly on their way. No force on earth seemed adequate to withstand the energy which was driving those mountains of water.

Often, thinking of those waves, I realize that life is very much like that troubled sea. Many small problems or waves arise to annoy and frighten us. Then, as the winds of adversity begin to blow, those small waves seem to unite to form huge swells that toss our little barks to and fro.

It is at such times that Christ's offer to give us rest is most needed and appreciated. It can be quite futile for us to buck some of these storms and to pit our puny strength against their force.

Many Christians wonder about the nature of the Rest Jesus offers to us today. Is it a mental state? Is it merely a spiritual condition or an emotional feeling? Is it some sort of theoretical fleeting thing that we claim to have by faith even when our spirits are not really at rest? Just how real is it? Is it practical in this rough and tumble world, or does it border on brainwashing one's self, through the power of suggestion, to pretend everything is all right when it really isn't?

During a recent Bible study, a dear saint, partly in jest, asked, "Just how do I rest in the Lord, fight the good fight, lie down in green pastures, run the race, walk beside the still waters, and endure the storm, all at the same time?" The answer is, of course, that we don't do them all—at the same time. But experience teaches us that each of these different facets of the Christian life, at one time or another, will be our own experience as God leads us along. Even though they sound contradictory, to the person who has learned to rest, each condition is harmonious with all the rest. One day God might have us resting peacefully, as in a wide pasture; the next moment he may ask us to stand alone in a storm and trust him. We had to learn this lesson in the occupation we chose for ourselves.

Buying property and owning the equipment connected with our business venture thrust upon our family many responsibilities and problems. Since the dedication of our business to the Lord, and our asking him to manage it to his glory, all kinds of destructive pressures and personal responsibilities I once felt necessary to manage our enterprise began to lift.

We knew we were to be occupying until he comes (Luke 19:13)—*in* the world but *not of* the world (John 17:14). After making this business commitment, we did not know how to stand aside so that Christ could have free access to direct its operation according to his wisdom. Normally the minds God designed for us function something like computers. Unless current data can be related to previously recorded information, our computer minds whirl and clang and sputter, but can't assimilate the new data. When God asks us to move in ways that are new to what we have become accustomed to, our minds don't know how to relate to the new direction.

It is not normal for the natural man to trust God in areas that are new to him. Our tendency is to pause long enough to analyze the situation, and attempt to relate it to some previous experiences. But as we shall see, God, because he is God, does not always work within the confines of human reason, or economic laws, or even scientific laws *as we know them.* We learned this during a situation we faced several years ago.

About seven years ago, we built a huge fiberglass super-slide at our recreation park in Winfield. First we had to design the molds, the forms from which the manufacturer later built the sections for the slide. When this phase of the construction was completed, we set up the slide in the park, and the molds we stored away at the factory for possible future use.

About a year ago, a man inquired about the possibility of using our forms to make a similar slide for his own amusement park. We discussed some of the details but reached no final agreement. I didn't even bother to mention it to Dorothy.

Then one night I dreamed that I found a pouch in which

were hidden some small stones resembling diamonds. In my dream, I took the stones to a jeweler, who confirmed that they were real gems and worth a lot of money. After examining one gem he placed it on the counter in front of me. As I reached for it, it was suddenly gone. Then I noticed that the other stones in the pouch had also disappeared. Thinking that someone must have played a sleight-of-hand trick on me, I looked around but there was no one in sight. Then I awoke with a deep sense of panic and loss.

Just as I awakened, Dorothy turned toward me and eyed me sleepily and said, "Samuel, I have a feeling you ought to check on those slide forms you have stored away at the fiberglass factory."

Dorothy and I hadn't discussed these molds for nearly seven years, and it seemed very strange to me that she should awaken out of a sound sleep and inquire about them before she was even fully awake.

As I told her about my dream, we began to wonder if God might not be warning us that something had happened to our forms. Perhaps the Lord could more easily bypass our mental computers and our roadblocks of rationality by speaking to our minds before they had awakened completely.

When the Lord prompts me to do something, even though it seems quite foreign to my previous learning, I've learned to respond. My reasoning, based on earlier experience, would tend to reject God's instructions, because they seem contrary to my understanding of the right thing to do. But when I obey God, he usually allows me to see the reason for what he asks me to do. Certainly, there were biblical precedents to this principle.

When God commanded Moses to cross the Red Sea, and Joshua to march around Jericho to claim victory, and Gideon to defeat the Midianites with a mere three hundred men, they were being asked to act contrary to what their minds had experienced. Yet God gave each a triumphant answer. We also, when we allow God to be totally in control in our situation, can accomplish his will through our acts of obedience.

Many of us, however, run into trouble when God chooses to direct us in what seems contrary to the way we are used to going or doing things. We tend to limit God to our own ability to understand. When he tries to break us away from the principles we learned in the natural world, we feel threatened. We would prefer to be led in comfortable ways that we can understand. Instead of allowing our reason to become subject to God, we try to make God subject to the finite limits of our understanding.

But the way of faith is God's road map for the Christian. Paul emphasized the importance of faith in God, in whatever he says to us: "Whatsoever is not of faith is sin" (Rom. 14:23). In another place, he wrote: "Because the carnal mind is enmity against God: for it is not subject to the law of God, neither indeed can be" (Rom. 8:7).

How reasonable was it to ask the Israelites to walk into the Jordan River like an army of lemmings in a death march to the sea? How reasonable was it to send Gideon against the armies of Midian with three hundred men with pitchers and lamps as their only weapons? Yet the result of each of these ventures of faith provides the answer to the questions.

Entering into God's Rest requires childlike faith, which could be the reason Jesus said, "Except ye . . . become as little children ye shall not enter into the kingdom of heaven" (Matt. 18:3).

We may criticize Israel for their lack of faith, but we should check ourselves to see whether we do any better in similar circumstances when God asks us to act according to faith rather than sight. God is the same yesterday, today, and forever. He is the same God today as he was in Gideon's day, and for that reason, he can perform the same kind of miracles today.

A person must learn to trust God's directions and obey, not only when his instructions agree with our previous experiences, but even when they do not. Unless we believe

God's Word more than we believe the evidence of our own senses, we do not really believe his Word. When Jesus called Peter to walk on the water, Peter could have reasoned that such an act was not scientific, and that it couldn't possibly work. But Peter defied the laws of science, as he knew them, and because he believed Jesus' words, he did the impossible. Peter could walk on water only after Jesus told him to do so. It was Jesus' word that kept him afloat. But when he stopped trusting Jesus' words and became concerned about what he could see—he looked at the waves—he began to sink.

It was not until I broke under the strain of work that I, like Peter, learned how to turn my life over to the Lordship of Christ. I had often asked God to help me, but God is not primarily interested in being our assistant—or coming to our aid whenever we get into trouble. It has been well said that "Jesus will be Lord of all or he is not Lord at all."

One of the subtle traditions that has infiltrated Christian thinking from paganism is the idea that "the gods" are here to help men. Jesus is not our valet, waiting to meet our needs just because we are Christians. Either he is in charge, or we are. His command is that we come to him and rest. One of the terms under which God will accept those who desire to come to him is that we rest when we get there.

If we do not fully trust him to take complete charge of our affairs, we do not meet the terms of entering his Rest under the new covenant. It is an absolute requirement that we rest from our labors in order that we may appropriate the full blessing of our new relationship to him.

People are often led to accept Jesus as Savior, but seldom are they taught how to make him Lord of their life. This partly explains why there are so many Christians with stunted growth. They are born into the family of God, but then little attention is paid to the maturing process required to make them act like sons and daughters of the King.

Dorothy and I were certain that morning that we should take some action, but we weren't exactly sure what it would be. At nine o'clock that morning, when I phoned the factory and inquired about the molds, I was told that someone had removed them several days earlier.

"I thought you authorized it," the plant manager apologized.

Dorothy and I began to pray, asking God to show us what we should do. Following a series of nudges which we felt were from the Lord, Dorothy and I spent the day tracing down those forms and making proper arrangements for their use. We discovered that just the day before I had had that dream, the gentleman who removed our molds from the factory had placed an order with another company to build a slide, using our forms. When God is in control, there is nothing to fear, because he knows all the secrets of men and he cannot fail.

Having begun the adventure in the Spirit, we were determined not to ruin it by turning to the flesh. We continued to look to God, and in no way attacked the man or reprimanded him for what he had done. We recognized that it could have been a misunderstanding, but as it was, he was taking advantage of the work we had done to make the forms and wasn't appearing to let us profit from his use of them. He needed a slide, and we needed the money, so we agreed to believe God for some financial gain from the situation, and for some benefit to everyone concerned. Several times a day for the next few days, Dorothy and I prayed about the problem.

Three days later, we started the morning as usual, having a time of prayer. Again we asked God to undertake about the mold forms and in faith thanked God for the answer.

We were still praying when we heard a knock on the door. I wondered who would be calling so early in the morning. There at the door was the man we were praying for, and in his hand was the check for the money we were praying about!

"I just wanted to give this to you," he said.

Once again we bowed our heads and thanked the Lord for

his care over us. We wondered if this kind of experience shouldn't be the rule rather than the exception in our daily affairs.

God had caused us to rest in his provision and care. A touchy situation that could have developed into an ugly crisis was resolved in a pleasant way for all of us. The man got his slide, and we received the money we were due, which we so much needed at that time.

The Lord's kindness in dealing with us was revealed several weeks later when we were invited to an evangelistic dinner meeting. We arrived a bit late, and the banquet hall was nearly full. We were pleased to see a friend who had reserved the seats for us waiting for us at the door ready to usher us to our places.

As we settled into our seats in the dining room, I thought I should get acquainted with the other people at our table. I could hardly believe my eyes! Seated on my left was the man with whom I had the dealings over the slide forms. How could it have "just happened"? It turned out to be that man's first experience in such a meeting—perhaps his first real opportunity to hear a clear presentation of the gospel. Words cannot express how happy I was that we had allowed God to handle the whole business transaction from start to finish. I wondered how I could have faced the man if I had related to him with anger or an accusing spirit. And what a poor testimony I would have been to the saving power of Christ!

When God warned us that our property had been tampered with, we could easily at that point have taken matters into our own hands and confronted the man with accusations and "put him in his place," so to speak. Such a course would likely have gained us an enemy, ruined the sale, and destroyed our witness. But when God begins a work, he is well able to finish it without interference or help from us. It seems evident that the principle of Galatians 4:3 applies to business management as well as other areas of life: "Having begun in the Spirit, are ye now made perfect in the flesh?"

Too many times, after God begins to do a supernatural work in our lives, we are inclined to take the matter out of his hands and attempt to complete it ourselves. In that way, many of the things God would do for us are never realized in our lives. God is well able to do what he starts, and when he begins to work, blessing will come unless we get in the way, and try to take control ourselves.

To keep God in control—to make him the Lord of our lives, the captain of our ships, we must learn to respond with trust. We must dare to let go of the helm so that he can take over. Anything short of total reliance is not real faith in God. Rest is a by-product of faith. The quality of rest we can experience is determined by the degree to which we can trust God with the unknown.

Jesus did not take charge of the boat on the Sea of Galilee until Peter was ready to let go of the controls himself. When Peter admitted that he wasn't equal to the problem, Jesus took over and stilled the storm. He then returned the boat's control to Peter.

Once Jesus' position as Captain of the ship was clearly defined in Peter's mind, and Jesus could rely on him to trust and obey without reference to previous experience, Peter could begin to rest in the Lord. The credit for a safe voyage would no longer go to Peter as the able seaman. The Lord, who assumes responsibility for our safety, is due the credit.

During the storm, Peter learned something new about trust. It is when God allows the winds to blow that we realize we need to trust him the most. When we flow with the sea, and learn how to utilize the force of the storm to advantage, then what was intended by the enemy to hurt us can actually be turned to our good, as it did for Peter and the other disciples, who learned a great lesson about faith in the Lord's ability to deliver.

Few settings can be more beautiful than the oceanside. We once enjoyed several days in Hawaii, during which time we would watch the surfers ride the waves off the coast. Huge breakers would roll in, and up on the waves would ride the surfers, flowing gracefully and easily with the swells. The surfers never fought against the force of those swells. They would climb onto their boards and position themselves on the front of the cresting wave, then would gently glide utilizing its mighty energy to thrust them along on an exhilarating ride toward the shore.

In the same way, Jesus asks us to stop fighting against the storms that crash in and to ride the waves. He wants us to seek to find out the reason he has allowed the waves to come crashing in, remembering that many lessons are taught during the storm. Once he gets our attention so that we will listen to what he would tell us, then the storm will have done its work, and can no longer affect us. As we trust Jesus, and by praise verify our trust in him, he will either guide us safely through the gale or he will utter his "Peace, be still!" to the stormy sea we sail.

On the Sea of Galilee, Jesus spoke the word and there was a great calm. But later, in another storm, Paul was shipwrecked in the Mediterranean and tossed onto the shore of the Isle of Melita. As a result of that storm and the shipwreck, the entire island population had the opportunity to hear the gospel. God's purpose was realized in Paul's shipwreck just as much as it was in the stilling of the storm on the Sea of Galilee.

Unless we learn how to read God's purpose in the storms that he allows to blow, we may find ourselves tossed helplessly to and fro onto the rocks of doubt and fear. Sometimes God wants to stir us up that he might mature us. When God wants to raise us up to a higher spiritual plane, we are inclined to resist because we have become too comfortable with the level of victory he has previously given. He may then allow a storm to arise that will not respond to the methods we had become accustomed to using. We ask God to calm the storm and nothing happens. We continue to pray, day after day, and nothing happens. And so we settle into a long dark valley of sorrow and perplexity. The deep tunnels between the swells can prove an awesome adventure, especially if we think we are all alone.

But how can we know the will of God—whether we should ask God to still the storm or to pray for strength to endure it? Some think that if they only had enough faith, they could calm every storm that blows up. If that were the case, Jesus would not have needed to suffer the storms of persecution as he did. Paul would not have been shipwrecked on the island of Melita. John would not have allowed himself to be a prisoner on Patmos, or Paul in Rome or Philippi. The apostles would not have allowed themselves to endure scourgings repeatedly, and Stephen would not have been stoned. The early Christians need not have become food for the lions and entertainment for the heathen in Roman arenas. In every one of these cases of endurance, the glory of God was magnified and the witness of God's Word made effectual through the storm that was endured. There is victory in calming the sea, but there is also a tremendous victory in enduring the storm and emerging with the banner of Christ held high to the glory of God.

The writer of Hebrews spoke of that kind of endurance:

> Others had trial of cruel mockings and scourgings, yea, moreover of bonds and imprisonment: they were stoned, they were sawn asunder, were tempted, were slain with the sword: they wandered about in sheepskins and goatskins; being destitute, afflicted, tormented; (of whom the world was not worthy:) they wandered in deserts, and in mountains, and in dens and caves of the earth. And these all, having obtained a good report through faith, received not the promise: God having provided some better thing for us, that they without us should not be made perfect.
> [Hebrews 11:36-40]

A "good report," in essence, is the confession that "our God is able." Whether we see the reward in this life or not, we know it is certain because God cannot fail to fulfill his promise. The Word of God is sure. It cannot fail! Daniel's three friends had their faith anchored more in the faithfulness of God than in physical deliverance (Dan. 3:17, 18).

Paul went to Rome to preach Christ. The Romans put him in jail and thought that would end his influence. Paul could have pined away, or he could have prayed that the jail doors would fly open. But no. When Paul was imprisoned with Silas at Philippi, they filled the midnight silence with hymns of praise, an earthquake literally shook the prison doors off, and Paul was set free. Now, in Rome, the same Paul was in jail again, but he was not released this time until God's purpose for him in that confinement was accomplished.

We learn in retrospect that out of that period of confinement came forth the books of Ephesians, Colossians, Philippians, Philemon, and possibly others. That is the way God works. Paul could never have accomplished in his lifetime of itinerant preaching the amount of good that was realized through his writings. Paul was flowing with the waves and rested as the storm of persecution blew. He knew that if God allowed him to remain in prison it would be because God wanted him to be closed in for a specific reason. Paul called himself "the prisoner of the Lord" (Eph. 4:1). He was not a prisoner of Rome as the Romans thought. God was using his Roman confinement as a writer's studio where he could meet with Paul and give him the inspiration for the Scriptures that have blessed millions.

The well-known verse describes this viewpoint:

Two men looked out through the selfsame bars;
One saw mud, the other saw stars.

God wants to show us how to relate to the storms that blow up in our lives. The first way to face them is to admit they are too much for us and that we don't know why they have come. The second key is to simply relax and recognize that God does know. The third key is to trust him to reveal his will to us in his own way and in his time. The fourth key is to rest, flow with the waves, and follow the leading of his Spirit, giving praise even before we know whether the victory will come when the storm is calmed or we find strength to endure it.

Thank God for peaceful green pastures. And thank him

also for stormy, turbulent seas, where his grace and goodness are just as available and where some of the greatest blessings flow out from our experience to bring calmness to other lives floundering in the storm.

9
God's Garden—A Place to Rest

Several years ago, I was in my study praying, meditating, and looking to God for direction. That morning, a dreamlike story was impressed on my mind.

I realized later that God was, in a rather unusual way, allowing me a preview of a process that was already beginning to take place within me. In my thoughts, it was as if I were standing on a knoll in a wild, desertlike place. I was hungry and very tired. The surrounding landscape was barren and depressing. I felt lonely, empty—as though no one in the world cared if I lived or died. The chilly, damp evening air penetrated my shabby clothes and I shivered in the wind.

As darkness began to settle in among the low bushes where I stood, the prospects of spending another unsheltered night in the open wastelands filled me with dread.

Then, I saw on the horizon some bright lights. They were coming from what appeared to be a sparkling city, so beautiful that it appeared to belong to another world far beyond earthly reach.

I made my way toward this breathtaking sight. In my heart, I longed to get into the city, but another part of me felt that I didn't belong in such luxurious surroundings. Travel-worn, weary, and shabby as I appeared, there would be no point in knocking at the huge entrance gate at which I stood. The city was walled, and the shining pathway that led to its gate obviously was for the more fortunate. If a person was really worthy, it appeared there would be no hindrance to getting in, but I felt I certainly was not one of them.

As I gazed upon the beauty of the place, I thought I would sneak up and get a better look. I thought perhaps I might get a better idea of what to do.

Carefully, in the twilight, I drew closer. The high, protecting wall surrounded the city, offering a certain sense of security, and I hoped to explore unobserved outside its borders. Taking every precaution, I crouched low and hurried along. Passing an open grating in the entrance gate, I stole a glimpse of the beautiful gardens inside.

The contrast between the clean interior, the neat walkways and flower beds, and my shabby condition was enough to make me want to turn away in sickly fear. I felt like a beggar, standing outside Buckingham Palace, longing to get inside but knowing there was no hope of gaining admission. I just knew I didn't belong in such a place. Any beggar knows he doesn't belong in a palace.

Fully convinced in my mind that there was no use trying the front gate, I continued my search, walking along the wall, hoping to find another way in. After exploring for some distance, I discovered a beaten path to an opening that looked like what might once have been a service entrance. Though it appeared not to be in regular use, the worn path showed that people were using the entrance. The path was steep, and the opening hard to reach, but obviously others had made it, and it looked worth the effort. Watching for an opportunity when no one might be looking, I sneaked through the opening without being seen.

Once inside the walls, I dashed for cover beside some of the beautiful young evergreens. The sight before me was more than I had anticipated. I had no idea the place could be so beautiful. In the center of the garden was a magnificent palace. Just looking at it made me tremble with excitement and fear. I knew I had never seen anything so wonderful in my life. I didn't know what to do next.

I was certain that in order for me to stay, I would have to get permission from the one who owned or controlled this place, but I felt far too unworthy even to try.

Surrounded by the beauty of that city, I felt a complete misfit. I dreaded the inevitable moment when I would be discovered and would be dealt with as an intruder. I hoped that if I did get caught, they would do nothing worse than throw me back out into the cold and darkness outside the walls. Hiding among the shrubs, I finally thought up a plan that might enable me to stay.

Nearby was a beautifully landscaped flower garden. Growing there were many kinds of plants in various states of maturity. Some were in full bloom, others were budding, and still others were going to seed. Around them, opening the soil were some fresh greet shoots that looked like weeds invading the flower bed.

I thought that if I could just show myself useful and really prove my worth, maybe I could be taken as a worker in the master's garden and be allowed to stay. Excited by my own brilliant idea, I walked to the nearest flower bed and began to uproot some of the plants that looked like weeds. I had been working only a few minutes when I felt a hand on my shoulder,

"What are you doing here and who are you?" a firm voice demanded.

Startled, I turned to look into the face of a very authoritative-looking man. I was speechless.

"Why did you pull those plants?" he asked.

"I only wanted to be helpful," I stumbled. "They looked like weeds. I'm sorry if I did anything wrong."

"Come with me," he commanded, and led me directly toward the palace.

I was petrified. I feared the very worst would happen to me. Why didn't he just throw me out and get it over with? Where would he take me? What would they do with me? Helplessly I followed along.

The man of authority stopped at the palace door where he summoned the attendant. This gentle-looking man gave me a comforting look and ushered me right into the presence of the master himself. In the tenderness and warmth of the master's smile, the icy fears suddenly melted away.

"Tell me about yourself," he gently encouraged. "Why did you come here, and how did you get in?"

"I was out there in the cold," I began. "Suffering from hunger and fatigue, and fearing I couldn't withstand the pressures of that lonely life much longer, I decided to come here in hope of finding refuge."

"But how did you get inside?" he asked.

"When no one was looking, I slipped in through an opening in the side wall," I confessed. "I thought it was a service entrance."

"Why did you not come in at the main gate?"

"I was afraid to. I thought I would be turned away. I had nothing to offer you, no money—not even a gift. Besides, the place looked too nice, and I looked so shabby. I didn't feel I belonged here as a guest. I wanted to impress you with my ability as a workman and hoped you would understand that I really am willing to work hard as a dedicated person. I don't expect something for nothing. In return for your giving me shelter here, I will gladly work for you faithfully for as long as you like."

"What work were you doing in my flower garden? Do you realize that in those few moments you uprooted some of my best plants? Is this a sample of your ability, appreciation, and dedication?"

"I am sorry, sir. Tending your garden seems much different from working in the one I was used to. I thought they were weeds. In my desperation, I thought that if I could contribute something to the welfare of this place, then I would more likely be recognized as having some potential for good, and might be allowed to stay."

The attendant was standing by—the one who had met me at the door as I entered the palace. The master did not have to say a word, for he seemed to understand as though they were one in thought and purpose. As he led me to an adjacent room, my whole life seemed to pass before me. I felt the wretchedness of my past and the emptiness of my future. Surrounded by such splendor, I loathed the rags in which I was dressed. At that moment the attendant asked for my old clothes. I took off the dirty rags and he led me to where I was bathed. I had never felt so clean before. Then he brought me some clean clothes and dressed me in as fine an outfit as I had ever seen.

Showered with all this kindness, I still did not feel comfortable. I was now so indebted to the master for his goodness that I feared there would be no way that I could repay him.

Next, I was taken to the dining room where a great banquet table was prepared for many people. It was laden with the most appealing and appetizing foods imaginable. After enjoying a full meal, I was returned to the master's great reception hall.

Feeling obligated, I immediately began to thank him for his kindness. In the same breath, I again began to offer him my services for what he had done for me.

"Listen," he began, "I don't need your services. In fact, the less you try to do around here, the better it will be for all of us. Whatever you touch, we will have to retouch. Whatever you do, we will have to undo. Whatever you try to fix, we will only have to correct. The best help you can be is to do nothing. Simply rest, enjoy yourself, and learn about me. If you appreciate what I can do for you, receive it with thanksgiving."

"But I feel so helpless and restless just being still. Can't I do something to express my gratitude to you for giving me a haven from the cold world outside?"

"No," he replied. "Rest, eat the food provided, and enjoy the shelter you have under my roof. My reward is to watch you grow and gain your strength, and to see you enjoy and delight in what I am doing for you.

"You see," he continued, "even if you tried to work in my garden, you would only do harm because you do not yet understand the methods by which we work, nor the principles by which we live in this place. You do not recognize a weed from a good plant. I want you to accept all that I have as yours. I want you to rest and learn to receive my peace in your heart. I am more interested in you than in anything you might do for me."

Then looking toward the entrance gate, which had seemed so formidable to me before, he added, "There is only one gate by which one should try to enter this place. Those who have courage, and by faith, knock and ask to be allowed inside are accepted into my city and are treated as my sons. Some like yourself lack the necessary faith, and seek to enter in by another way. Anyone doing this is really acting like a thief or a robber. Those who seek admittance by the service entrance like you did are met by the man of authority whose name is Law. His work is to bring such as yourself to me. He is also known as the Schoolmaster, for his job is to show people like you how useless it is to try to earn your entrance to this place. As soon as you do something wrong trying to please me, he points it out and brings you to me.

"People like yourself feel better if they can compensate for my kindness. Even though you may not realize it, those folks belong to the class of people called Legalists, because they want to prove their appreciation for my kindness by what they think they can do after they enter in. They seek to prove their love to me by their works. I judge them not alone by what they do (for their righteousness is only as filthy rags) but by what they are. Those who enter by the service entrance must cease from their own works, and must accept the goodness of this place by faith or they can't stay."

Suddenly the gate, which appeared so fearsome and formidable, looked warm and inviting. Why hadn't I been more trusting and believing in the goodness of the master?

EARNING REST

The story illustrates many truths about God and man. For years I tried to make myself worthy of the kingdom through my own efforts. Entering into God's Rest is something we do by faith, and as the story illustrates, nothing we can do once we enter in can ever make us worthy enough to stay. God doesn't expect us to involve ourselves in legalistic activity to earn our keep. Grace is never earned or it wouldn't really be grace.

Those who try to please God and make themselves acceptable to God are like the Galatians of Paul's day. They sought security in claiming to obey the ten commandments. Some of them today even seek a return to the Mosaic Sabbath, often referring to certain verses in Hebrews chapter four in support of their doctrine:

> For he spake in a certain place of the seventh day on this wise, And God did rest the seventh day from all his works. And in this place again, If they shall enter into my rest. Seeing therefore it remaineth that some must enter therein, and they to whom it was first preached entered not in because of unbelief: . . . There remaineth therefore a rest to the people of God. [Heb. 4:4-6, 9]

Their argument runs something like this: Verse four speaks of the seventh day in which God rested from his creative works. Verses five and six indicate that God's people should enter into the Rest which God has been offering to us since the beginning of the world. And verse nine says that there remains a Rest or *sabbatismos* for the people of God in our own day. Then because the Greek word, *sabbatismos,* refers to the Sabbath of creation week which remains to our day, these verses seem to show that Sabbath observance today is as obligatory and required in our time just as it was in Moses' day.

Even though the above line of reasoning may seem on the surface to be valid, a close study of this passage indicates that this is not the only possible interpretation or the most likely interpretation of the passage. Those who insist that theirs is the only valid answer to any spiritual question are responsible for many of the divisions that have occurred within the body of Christ. Rather than study the Scriptures to find support for our divisive doctrines, it is time we first see what the Scriptures teach and subject ourselves to the uniting influence of the written Word, which will result in a coming together among God's people.

A study of the Bible based primarily on human ability to reason it out has split the once united body of Christ into hundreds of denominations and sects. When we approach God's Word with our chief dependance upon the Holy Spirit to teach us, the results are more unifying and profitable. Just as God's Word was not given by human reason, so its understanding is not by human reasoning (2 Pet. 1:20, 21). As we have mentioned earlier, because spiritual things are spiritually discerned (1 Cor. 2:14), it is not possible to determine the true meaning of God's Word by analyzing it only with the natural mind. Only as the Holy Spirit abides within us can he teach us so that what we learn is truth. With this in mind, we turn again to our study of Hebrews chapter four.

God has created for man's benefit, as illustrated by the story and reiterated many times in the Scriptures, a Sabbath Rest. It is not only available today, but must be entered into by all who wish to maintain a life in Christ. In the passage in Hebrews, the writer does not call men to attach any special significance to Saturday or to any other specific day of the week. The day he emphasized is the day which is called "today" in Hebrews 4:7.

The day when the Holy Spirit calls us to rest from our

labors and to enter into God's provision, is the day in which we are given opportunity to respond. Tomorrow may not be ours. Even as Felix (Acts 24:25) delayed and was lost, so many in our time are lost because they fail to respond in the day when the Spirit calls.

God's Sabbath was begun at creation. It was interrupted by sin. Its blessing was dimmed as man was condemned to work for his livelihood. It was restored again by the death and resurrection of Christ, and continues on unbroken for all who enter into it by faith. Only as we cease from our own works and striving can we enter into his Sabbath Rest. After God completed all the work of creation, he attached a special significance to the seventh day because that was the day in which man first entered into God's Rest. It was a time of jubilation in heaven and on earth. All creation joined in honoring God for having created a setting which provided a Sabbath, or atmosphere, capable of giving to man total rest and trust in God.

The heavenly Father was mindful to provide ahead of time for all his children's necessities. No effort was spared by God to make Eden the ideal home for his creation. The great celebration which God initiated on the seventh day did not cease twenty-four hours later, but continued as long as man, the newest of the Creator's achievements, honored his Maker by acknowledging that God's provision was perfect.

Later, the seventh day was significant to Israel because it was symbolic of the day when God opened the way for man to enter into his total Rest in Eden. Rather than seeing the partial rest on the seventh day as a symbolic reminder of the total Edenic Sabbath, they made it an end in itself as though the mere cessation from activity could give them favor with God. They failed to enter into God's provision but continued with the symbol of that provision (Heb. 3:17-19).

To honor the work of the original creation, God gave to Israel a certain day—the seventh day of the week. To honor Christ's work of re-creation and redemption which he finished on the cross, God expanded the blessing earlier attached to the seventh day and extended it to cover all time.

Israel could enter into rest once a week only. Now we may enter into God's Rest any day of the week. Indeed, we must not only enter in, but must abide in it continuously if we truly wish to honor the Sabbath of the Lord our God.

The writer of Hebrews speaks of the Sabbath of creation as a present and continuing experience. He does not tell his audience to wait until the seventh day of the week before entering into God's Rest. Indeed, he calls them to enter immediately while it is still "today." Because God's Sabbath Rest is not limited to the seventh day, it is evident that one may enjoy the blessings of God's Rest without regard to one special day of the week. The symbol ended at the cross only to make way for the substance (Rom. 14:4-6).

The Sabbath is a spiritual reality and must be seen as a continuing relationship with God. It now speaks of an abiding in the finished work of Christ rather than a mere cessation from vocational activity.

Through sin, man forfeited the Edenic Rest. Then through Israel's experience, God demonstrated that man does not have the capacity to regain that Rest on his own. Christ's death was the only way by which God could once again restore to man that which he had lost. Without the cross, the Sabbath was gone beyond recall. The point of beginning again—the true birthday of the world—can no longer be seen as relating to the first Adam, but to the second Adam who restored God's Rest—full and complete—after the original pattern and not after the abbreviated Mosaic rest comprising only one-seventh of time. One may cease from all physical activity and still be destitute of God's Rest or the peace which Christ offers.

It is not until a person fills the void by entering into the Creator's provision of the cross and assimilates the blessings provided that he can truly be said to have found the Sabbath Rest. In Moses' day, God began to return the lost dominion to man by restoring to him first the physical necessities. The second and biggest step, to restore to him the spiritual kingdom was to be accomplished later when the promised Messiah would die to pay in full the penalty of man's sin.

Because Israel rebelled, God postponed their physical deliverance from the curse of sin. For the rest of their history, they would have to struggle under the curse by continuing to eat bread by the sweat of their faces. Instead of the Edenic Rest in which food, water, clothing, immunity from disease, and protection from all enemies would be solely God's responsibility, they were allowed only a symbol of that Rest on one day in seven. God gave Israel the seventh day Sabbath that they might not forget what he had planned to give them, and what they had rejected when he took them out of Egypt.

THE PROCESS REVERSED

In Hebrews we find God granting to us the same reprieve from the curse of sin, except that now the steps are reversed. Instead of granting us physical deliverance first, he offers the spiritual kingdom first. Because Christ has died and paid the full price for our sin, and has bought back the lost dominion, he can rightfully offer Rest to his people, and we can accept it by faith now! The order of our release from the curse of sin since the cross is: "Seek ye first the kingdom of God, and his righteousness, and all these things shall be added unto you" (Matt. 6:33).

Today, as we enter spiritual Rest, God has promised to add unto us the physical necessities also. Adding implies a gradual increase, one by one. A satisfactory spiritual relationship with God is a prerequisite to physical victory. The nearer we get to God, the more he fulfills his promises to us. We must cease striving to impress him with our attainments. As we do so, we find that our victory lies not in the partial rest of the fourth commandment, but in the Sabbath of the Creator which is designed to ultimately restore to us all our needs, whether spiritual or physical.

Lest there remain any misunderstanding as to what God requires today, Paul tells us not to lay stress on so-called holy days, or on the symbolic Sabbath as the Jews were required to do lest we also miss the mark.

> Who art thou that judgest another man's servant? to his own master he standeth or falleth. Yea, he shall be holden up: for God is able to make him stand. One man esteemeth one day above another: another esteemeth every day alike. Let every man be fully persuaded in his own mind. He that regardeth the day, regardeth it unto the Lord; and he that regardeth not the day, to the Lord he doth not regard it. He that eateth, eateth to the Lord, for he giveth God thanks; and he that eateth not, to the Lord he eateth not, and giveth God thanks. [Romans 14:4-6]

Paul further spoke of our release from these Old Testament ordinances:

> Therefore let no one sit in judgment on you in matters of food and drink, or with regard to a feast day or a new moon or a Sabbath. Such [things] are only the shadow of things that are to come, *and* they have only a symbolic value. But the reality—the substance, the solid fact of what is foreshadowed, the body of it—belongs to Christ. [Colossians 2:16, 17, Amp.]

It was not by accident that Paul wrote the words "but the reality—the body—belongs to Christ," at the end of verse seventeen. These words are not only part of verse seventeen, but are part of the sentence preceding them. Some consider this a superfluous ending to an otherwise good sentence. Paul was trying to contrast the symbolic practices of the Mosaic dispensation with the body or solid fact of what those symbols illustrated. Having lived out their purposes, the symbols of the truth must not be confused with the truth itself. Old Covenant symbols inserted into the New Covenant setting become a negative and confusing element.

Where the new begins, the old must end.

God doesn't change. What God gave to Adam in the beginning, and later reiterated to Abraham he still holds out to us as the only way to him. What he still later gave to Israel at Sinai, when they refused to trust him, was specifically for their time and was ordained to remain in effect only "until the Seed should come" (Gal. 3:19).

The whole Sinai episode with all its laws was developed because of the hardness of their hearts and unbelief. The heart of Paul's teaching seems to be that the external forms must not be allowed to become a polarizing influence among Christians. If some should feel that they should honor one particular day of the week, they should not be judged by the rest, but neither should they consider others who do not see as they do as any less in the will of God than themselves. If some believe they may honor a different day, or every day alike, God also honors and accepts that service to himself. Paul cautions Christians to be certain that their practices do not become a cause of division in the Body of Christ. No practice or belief that separates or divides members of the Body of Christ is condoned. Satan works to divide. Jesus came to unite.

COME AND REST

Man has responded to the curse brought upon the human race by Adam's sin by becoming defensive, and by seeking to compensate for his failure by good works. Man finds it hard to trust God for restoration. He has an inner need to prove himself. After six thousand years, he is still laboring under the burden of it.

But God sent his Son to take away the curse—that we might have abundant life. God's call is to all outside the gates of his city: "Come unto me, all ye that labour and are heavy laden, and I will give you rest. Take my yoke upon you, and learn of me; for I am meek and lowly in heart:

and ye shall find rest unto your souls" (Matt. 11:28, 29).

"And the Spirit and the bride say, Come. And let him that heareth say, Come. And let him that is athirst come. And whosoever will, let him take the water of life freely" (Rev. 22:17).

For further material on this subject write:

Sam and Dorothy Pestes
Site 34-16 R.R. 2
Winfield, B.C. V0H 2C0 Canada